Mary Happy

WISDOM ROADS

Enjoy —

Lawrence Muller

Wisdom Roads

Conversations with Remarkable Meditation Masters

Laurence Freeman
Swami Satchidananda
Tenzin Wangyal Rinpoche
Edward McCorkell
Swami Shankarananda
Shree Chitrabhanu
Wayne Teasdale
Bhante Gunaratana

by
Lawrence G. Muller

Continuum
New York   London

2000

The Continuum International Publishing Group Inc
370 Lexington Avenue, New York, NY 10017

The Continuum International Publishing Group Ltd
Wellington House, 125 Strand, London WC2R OBB

Printed in the United States of America

Library of Congress Cataloging-in-Publication Data

Muller, Lawrence G.
  Wisdom roads: conversations with remarkable meditation masters / by
Lawrence G. Muller.
     p.   cm.
  "Laurence Freeman, Swami Satchidananda, Tenzin Wangyal Rinpoche,
Edward McCorkell, Swami Shankarananda, Shree Chitrabhanu, Wayne
Teasdale, Bhante Gunaratana."
  Includes bibliographical references.
  ISBN 0-8264-1234-3 (pbk.)
  1. Meditation.   I. Freeman, Laurence.   II. Title.
  BL627.M85   2000
  291.4'35—dc21   99-057184

To Charan Singh, Bede Griffiths, and all the remarkable
meditation masters known and unknown,
past, present, and future, East and West.

To my mother, Rita,
and my father, Arthur,
for their lifelong love and support.

To Keiko, for her love,
that inspires and accompanies me
on the journey.

CONTENTS

ACKNOWLEDGMENTS

Though painfully aware that the gratitude the author wishes to express for the invaluable assistance in the making of this book is, in the end result, "beyond words," nevertheless, he has to give it a try.

Sufficient thanks can never be given to the following friends and colleagues in the work: to Harold McMullen, professor of education and philosophy at Lord Fairfax Community College in Virginia, for the many conversations and welcome advice over the years, and especially for his taking the lead in organizing the annual "Being Together" conferences over the last decade, which are co-sponsored by the monastic communities of the Bhavana Society and Holy Cross Abbey. Brother Benedict Simmonds OCSO is recalled for his vital, early support of the book. I also gratefully bow to the sannyasis of Yogaville, swamis Karunananda, Sharadananda and Hamsananda, and to Dayananda, the personal secretary of Swami Satchidananda, who did assuredly vouchsafe an ashram conversation on a cold January evening. Thanks also to David Rees at WCCM in London and Rosemary O'Connell in New York who ably facilitated my contact and meeting with Father Laurence Freeman at the House of the Redeemer in New York City. Additional thanks are also due to Mamata, who facilitated my meeting with Shree Chitrabhanu at the Jain International Meditation Center in New York. And closer to home in Virginia, I am grateful for the generous support of Becki Mosteller, Deborah West, Donna Cintron, Jackie Adams, Jayanne Bixby, Kim Bean, and Shirley Echelman at the reference desk of the Handley Regional Library in Winchester, Virginia, for their gracious assistance and support during the preparation of the final manuscript.

John Massie of Ligminch proved indispensable in advance of my meeting with Tenzin Wangyal Rinpoche. Noted author and educator Laura Robb has provided great enthusiasm and real guidance and friendship in this writer's journey.

A special word of thanks is also due to Ron Morris, managing editor of the *Winchester Star*, for his far-sighted support of religious news reporting and for launching the weekly religion feature during my time with the newspaper; and to editors Susan Burke, Wayde Byard, and Roger Hendrix for their editorial expertise.

My heartfelt salutations go out to Michael Fitzgerald of Winchester—poet, essayist, Baha'i, and friend-extraordinaire—who here is celebrated for his enthusiastic support in all matters literary and metaphysical. And above all, for our friendship that is now in its fifteenth year and past all counting.

Last but not least, my mother, Rita Muller, was there with me for the moment of clarity and inspiration that gave birth to this book called *Wisdom Roads*.

INTRODUCTION

Meditation is for everyone. It is the practical, experience-based wisdom that is at the core of all the religions and at the very heart of the spiritual life. Meditation is the essential art of self-mastery and right living. *Wisdom Roads* invites the reader to consider exploring the meditation roads in this book.

The book intends to shed some new light on meditation both for the experienced meditator and for those who are taking their first in-depth look at meditation spirituality. It aims to assist persons of faith in their quest to further deepen their spiritual life through meditation. Also, it should prove useful to the nonbeliever—who cannot accept, or subscribe to any organized religious doctrine—but who is curious about meditation. This book of conversations with meditation masters makes clear that each and every truth-seeker must answer the question for oneself: Do I want to make room for meditation in my very busy life? To this end, the book brings together, for the very first time under one cover, outstanding living teachers of meditation practice from quite diverse, yet very accessible, wisdom traditions. The reader will find contemplative prayer, Christian meditation and Christian Sannyasa, among the paths of Christian meditation; Theravada Vipassana and Bon Dzogchen within the broad field of Buddhist meditation; Jain meditation; and the practices of Kriya/Advaita Vedanta and Integral Yoga. It is generally understood that both the Christian and Yoga meditation traditions define the person, soul, or the *atman*/self within the context of a creator God, or the Absolute. In contrast, the Bon, Jain, and Theravada traditions are usually viewed as nontheistic roads to liberation or enlightenment.

It is in the silence of meditation that a meeting beyond the words and concepts of the religions becomes possible. The eight remarkable meditation masters have come together in this book to offer a plain-speaking, practice-oriented spirituality of meditation to sincere seekers of truth everywhere. Theirs is a very user-friendly approach to meditation. And their practical insights into the ongoing process that is the meditative life illuminate the various and particular forms of meditation practice. These are taught in the great meditation wisdom traditions of the religions.

They would be among the first to agree that when it comes to meditation, no one path or teaching has the answer for all. No one meditation practice can claim to be suitable for everyone. And yet they remind us that keeping faith—

which here means being faithful to the practice of meditation—we are advised to choose carefully among the many paths of meditation available. But then, having done so, in most cases we do well to stay and grow and deepen within the one we do choose. It is also better to approach meditation without expectations of instant results or grand visions.

For some of us, the term "masters" may give us pause. The word is used here to indicate a high degree of spiritual mastery, wisdom, and teaching expertise on the part of the meditation teachers. The actual practice and teachings—and not the personality of the teacher, as is seen in some guru-centered schools of meditation—remain the primary focus of these eight master meditation teachers. Their own exemplary mastery is only meant to guide, and serve as an example to their students, who must by their own steady efforts continue to walk along these meditation wisdom roads.

The meditation masters found in this book all seem to concur that the path of meditation continues to be a dynamic learning experience for each of them as well. A master can be seen on one level as the student who has learned his lessons well. The meditation wisdom teachers point us in the right direction. But they always emphasize that there is no substitute for direct experience on the part of the individual meditator.

This book is the fruit of talks, meetings, and encounters—in a word, conversations—with truly remarkable spiritual masters, or master meditators, over a number of years. It now seems inevitable to this writer and meditator that it should be so. Yet as always in things really important to one's life and intrinsic well being, there was also a fair amount of struggle, hard knocks, and false starts—in the process of making it a reality.

The book also represents then a gradual awakening of sorts for its author. It naturally grew out of my work for a number of years as a religion journalist at a daily newspaper in Virginia. Three stories from this period stand out in my mind in this regard. The first is an interview with a young California woman who was ordained as a Theravada Buddhist nun at the Bhavana Society Forest Monastery and Retreat Center in West Virginia. Another is the visit of Tibetan monks and nuns from India to Holy Cross Abbey, a Catholic monastery in Virginia. And the third is my own pilgrimage to a thousand-year-old Camaldolese Benedictine hermitage in Italy. I also ended up writing about that experience as a religion feature story.

Those earlier journalistic encounters had something of what the monk and writer Thomas Merton calls the "seeds of contemplation" about them.

This is the case with Bhante Gunaratana. I first met him a decade ago, and his progressive vision for the Bhavana community continues to guide its steady growth. Though I met Laurence Freeman and Shree Chitrabhanu in New York, and Tenzin Wangyal Rinpoche in Charlottesville, only for the first time last year, it is fair to say that these leading exponents of the Christian meditation, Jain, and Bon traditions already feel like old friends.

But on the other hand, I have known the Cistercian monk Father Edward McCorkell, who lives and teaches at the very same Holy Cross Abbey—where the Tibetans visited—for about ten years now. He is always available to lay retreatants at the monastery, many of whom are intent on learning and developing the practice of contemplative prayer. As a teacher, he utilizes the Cistercian insights of Thomas Keating and Thomas Merton. Also, Father Edward can certainly claim a deep understanding of, and long-term expertise in, the ongoing Christian dialogue with Buddhists and Hindus.

As it happens, my own personal Camaldolese Benedictine connection—I have been a Camaldolese lay oblate for the past eight years—and my journalistic reporting on the annual "Being Together" conferences held in Virginia, which recently marked their ninth anniversary, all played a part in my meeting with Brother Wayne Teasdale. He is a Christian sannyasi and leading disciple of Dom Bede Griffiths, who himself was both a sannyasi and Camaldolese Benedictine monk, and who was the guiding light of a Christian ashram in south India—Shantivanam Saccidananda Ashram—for some twenty-five years, until his death in 1993.

Several happy encounters with the wonderful sannyasis of Yogaville, both at their central Virginia ashram and at "Being Together," led eventually to my conversation with Swami Satchidananda, who this past year celebrated the fiftieth anniversary of his receiving Sannyasa. I also was fortunate to meet Swami Shankarananda, of the Divine Life Church of Absolute Oneness in Baltimore, during his period of teaching of Advaita Vedanta in the Shenandoah Valley.

The conversational nature of these interviews with the eight *Wisdom Roads* meditation masters seeks above all to contribute to that spirit of dialogue among the world religions and spiritual traditions. The book also celebrates the value and importance of deep abiding friendship on the meditative journey. These eight meditation masters must be counted among the "soul friends" who help us recharge our spiritual batteries, as we continue to walk the spiritual path. Without such friendships, it seems that all too often the journey—the process, the experience of the meditative life—turns into a very dry and lifeless affair indeed.

Meditation in its fullest sense encompasses the whole of life—what one hesitates to characterize as "nonmeditative" activities. In fact, it reaches well beyond the perimeters of a daily sitting meditation practice. Meditation helps develop the right attitude of mind toward the events of life. It seeks to balance contemplation and action, or being and doing.

The conversations discuss the essentially complementary roles of teacher and student in the practice of meditation; the need for community; and what the good life and the good death are. The meditative consciousness moves us to alleviate the suffering of Tibet that Wayne Teasdale invokes. It embraces the feminine dimension in the Christian trinity that Edward McCorkell explores; the easily doable one-minute meditation Bhante Gunaratana offers; the problem of the media culture which Swami Satchidananda analyzes; the dangers of spiritual materialism Swami Shankarananda warns about. Also, Laurence Freeman assures us children are born meditators. Tenzin Wangyal elucidates the Bon approach to death. Shree Chitrabhanu looks beyond formal religious institutions, as the Jain way seeks to contribute to the peaceful transformation of the world.

In the course of these conversations, it becomes clearer to us how these meditation guides are so well grounded in their own tradition. All genuine meditation masters bring an open hearted, friendly approach—call it one of "spiritual humanism"—in the encounter with the world religions and wisdom traditions. Their main work is to set us on the road to self-mastery.

The student's role is to learn to see by way of the clear meditative prism. So that we begin to enter into that silent inner conversation, as we move through a concentrated observing, waiting, listening, and witnessing to our innermost being. A meditation practice brings us into a deeper understanding of what it means to be human beings. We are spiritual beings who are learning how to live well in a human incarnation. Still, the wisdom teachers advise us that it is a very gradual process. They help us to begin and stay the course. We ourselves must walk the meditation road. Even the great spiritual masters cannot save us from ourselves and our cherished illusions. As we practice meditation, the ego must daily let go of even its subtlest, most rarefied, even spiritual, pretensions.

I have my own personal testament in light of these perennial truths. For me, it was literally an uphill climb to see Bede Griffiths seven years ago in northern California. I can look back now—as if with a "Buddha half-smile"—on the assorted wrong turns I made: my getting off at the commuter train station before the one I needed; to be followed by my catching a bus to narrow the distance between myself and the aptly named Mercy Center, where Father Bede was scheduled to speak.

I saw on the last leg of the journey how foolishly weighed down I was with an overfull backpack, even as I went up the notoriously steep hills of a San Francisco Bay area town. Truly, it is that much harder to reach for the heights when you're overloaded with stuff. Still rather amazingly, I did make it up that hill to where Bede was speaking that night. And, despite my doubting that I would ever get there, I was right on time to hear him as well.

What I took back down the mountain with me that late summer night in 1992 is the *darshan* of holiness, a glimpse of compassion and loving-kindness—or what Buddhists call *metta*—of Father Bede. He had found the treasure of meditation. He was eager to share it with everyone he could. Bede recounted his personal experience of being sustained in that nurturing, loving embrace of the Divine Mother, in the aftermath of his nearly fatal stroke a few years earlier. The account of his spiritual epiphany was made all the more poignant, given that he again took ill upon his return to the ashram in India. He died there the next year, 1993.

In the spirit of Bede Griffiths and all the great meditation masters past, present, and future, this book is an offering, a marker, a signpost on the way. We live in terribly wonderful times. There is really no need to wish we could have lived in the time of Jesus or Buddha, or some other great master. Not when, right now—and even as I write this—such accessible, open, and friendly master teachers are at hand to set us on the right and appropriate meditation wisdom path.

The time is now. Like meditation itself, this book of wisdom conversations aspires to be the spiritual traveler's boon companion for the open road.

CHRISTIAN MEDITATION WITH LAURENCE FREEMAN

L.M.: What is Christian meditation—or the way of the mantra—as initially rediscovered and taught by Father John Main? And now, by you through the World Community of Christian Meditation? As a corollary to that, why should one practice Christian meditation?

L.F.: That's a lot for one question. It's like one of those Chinese boxes, one inside the other. Well, Christian meditation is a tradition of Christian prayer—a practice of Christian prayer which John Main found, and recognized, and rediscovered—particularly in the teachings of the early Christian monks, of the desert fathers. I think that the first thing one should say is that meditation itself is a universal tradition. You find it in all the great religions. But I also think that, for the Western mind, and for the church today, we have lost touch with our own Christian tradition of meditation. And, we often assume that meditation is only an oriental tradition or practice.

It was Father John's experience that he first learned to meditate when he was in the East, some years before he became a monk. That experience probably helped him to recognize the practicality of the teachings on prayer—that he later found in the writings of John Cassian. He was one of the great communicators of the wisdom of the desert tradition.

L.M.: In the fourth century?

L.F.: The fourth and fifth centuries. And really, he was one of the great pillars of the western spiritual, contemplative tradition. Cassian devotes two of his conferences to prayer—numbers nine and ten. The ninth is about the theory of prayer; it's a very beautiful and rich description of the nature of prayer. But he doesn't say how to do it. In the tenth conference, he actually gives a method. The method he gives is to take a phrase, which he calls a formula, in Latin, and repeat that formula incessantly, continuously. He describes the repetition of this single phrase over and over in the mind and heart—as bringing us to that poverty of spirit—which is the first of the beatitudes. Now, John Main recognized this, not just as a theory, but as an actual practice. His teaching comes directly out of the wisdom of Cassian. You will find the same tradition in many of the other great teachers, including the author of *The Cloud of Unknowing*.

L.M.: The anonymous, fourteenth-century English mystic. I understand that when Father John first became a Benedictine, there wasn't any knowledge of the way of the mantra in his monastery in Britain. In fact, he had first learned of the mantra through a Hindu teacher he met in the East.

L.F.: When he first became a monk in the fifties, it was still a long time before meditation would become generally known.

L.M.: It took another decade, the sixties.

L.F.: Exactly, this was before before the great era of TM—Transcendental Meditation—and the Beatles, and the great influx of Eastern spirituality into the West. Most of the religious orders, including monastic orders, and all the seminaries, had effectively lost touch with that central tradition of Christian contemplative prayer. They had really got themselves restricted to mental prayer, discursive prayer, or meditation. When John Main became a monk, his novice master heard him describe the way of meditation he was following, which had brought him to the monastery. The novice master couldn't understand it, and he told Father John: "This was obviously the Lord's way of bringing you to the monastery. But now that you're here, you should abandon it and return to our Christian prayer."

L.M.: So he ordered Father John not to meditate?

L.F.: Well, he advised it.

L.M.: He advised against meditation.

L.F.: Those were the days when monks were still obedient; so he obeyed. Father John later said that when he came back to the practice of meditation through Cassian, he came back on God's terms, not his own. He saw that as a desert period, but also as a purifying, fruitful experience.

L.M.: Did your own reading of some of John Main's writings lead you to become a monk?

L.F.: Yes, I was led to be a monk directly through meditation; and through having Father John as a teacher. I had actually met him a long time ago, before I was even thinking of becoming a monk—when I was a boy in school. He was teaching school when I was about thirteen or fourteen. He wasn't teaching meditation at that point. That was my first encounter with him. And then we met again, in the late sixties, when he had started meditating again. He was at that time headmaster of a Benedictine school in Washington, D.C., Saint Anselm's. I was visiting there at Easter. And he introduced me to meditation.

I never doubted the rightness of the path, it just made sense to me. It was clear, it was simple, it was authentic. It was also a discipline—one that was quite challenging to me. I was then attending university, with many distractions and worries. So I practiced it very intermittently. Then, Father John came back to England, and he started a lay community centered on meditation at his monastery in London. The idea was that you would join the community for six months to receive instruction and training in meditation—and spiritual preparation for life. I joined that lay community. But because I am a very undisciplined and slow learner, I had to become a monk to learn it.

19

L.M.: It wasn't long thereafter that you made the commitment to monastic life.

L.F.: Yes, after the initial six months. I struggled with that. I had not intended to become a monk. It seemed to me to be the path to follow. For me anyway, the monastic life was the best way I could follow that path of meditation.

L.M.: One hopes that Christian meditation will have a real benefit for the majority of people in the church, for lay people living their lives out in the world. Are many parishes here in America encouraging Christian meditation practice?

L.F.: Well, there are now many parishes and religious communities and retreat houses where there are weekly group meetings. Also you'll find groups at places of work. There is one meeting here in New York, at the United Nations, that meets every week.

L.M.: They do the way of the mantra, or *maranatha*?

L.F.: Yes, they are following the tradition that John Main passed on. There are many other groups. There are contemplative groups in other traditions as well, such as Centering Prayer. So I think that there is a growth and awakening. It is mostly among lay people; the clergy, on the whole, are a little slow to tune into this. Though there certainly are wonderful priests and religious around the country who are deeply contemplative men and women. They teach and encourage lay people to teach meditation.

We recently had a school for teachers of meditation at our monastery in Pecos, New Mexico. Twenty-five people came from around the country. It was our first school for teachers in the U.S. There was perhaps one priest and two sisters, the rest were lay people. I was very excited and impressed by their depth and clarity; and, by their grasp of the teaching.

L.M.: Was Cassian's method then the practice of maranatha?

L.F.: No, Cassian suggested the repetition of a particular phrase from the Psalms, "Oh God, come to my assistance." That is the one which Saint Benedict took over for the opening verse of the Divine Office. John Main recognized Cassian's phrase to be like the mantra he had learned in the East. The basic teaching is that you choose a short word or phrase as your mantra, and that you repeat it continually. There are various phrases, words, or mantras that you could choose. The *Cloud* author suggests the word *God*, for example.

John Main felt that the word *maranatha* was a beautiful mantra for Christians, because it is the oldest Christian prayer. And it is in the Aramaic language that Jesus spoke. It is a scriptural word and prayer too, that Saint Paul ends the First Letter to Corinthians with. So it's a very suitable word. Also, the length and sound of the word are helpful in calming the mind. Another very ancient Christian mantra is the name of Jesus—which you find in the Jesus prayer tradition of the Eastern Orthodox Church.

L.M.: It's also found in *The Way of the Pilgrim.*

L.F.: The hesychast tradition developed rather later in the Christian church. But the same understanding of the praying of one word is very clear.

L.M.: How does one go about Christian meditation, including the basic posture and breathing?

L.F.: We don't—John Main and those of us who follow in his tradition—we don't so much emphasize the technique aspect of it. It is more a simple discipline—not easy, but simple. We emphasize very much the simplicity of the practice. We would say, sit down: sit still with your back straight. So that you are in an alert, faithful, and comfortable posture. That also helps you to breathe properly. Close your eyes lightly—relax—and then, silently, interiorly, begin to say your word, say your mantra. When thoughts come into the mind—as they will in great number—just ignore them. Don't fight with them, don't waste any energy getting into conflict with them.

L.M.: Don't analyze them.

L.F.: Don't analyze them, just let go. Whether they're holy thoughts, or not so holy thoughts. Just let them go, simply let that level of mental activity go. Then, by continually returning to the word, gently but faithfully, you are led through the distractions, thoughts, and images to a deeper center, which we call the heart. In that center, we discover the peace of Christ. We discover Jesus at prayer in us. Now at the time of meditation we are not theologizing about it, or thinking about it. But the fruits of that journey from the mind to the heart, are readily experienced in daily life, especially in our relationships.

L.M.: I was reading one of Father John's essays where he mentioned the simplicity, as you said, of the mantra. How perhaps that simplicity is exactly what contemporary men and women find so difficult, about almost anything. If there is simplicity, they're even skeptical about it.

L.F.: I think that's true. We are a very complex culture; we worship complexity. Look at the way we are with computers and everything. It is very difficult for us to trust simplicity. And yet we hunger for it, we thirst for it, we crave it. We realize how emotionally and psychologically complex we've become. Our society is incredibly complex, sometimes to the point of absurdity. How difficult it is to make a telephone call in the United States—I always annoy the operators by telling them that it is much easier to telephone in India. Even materially, the culture complicates our lives with all these consumer demands. And we are conditioned to be constantly stimulated by desire, and constantly buying. So I think we crave simplicity, and that is why there is such a deep turning toward meditation in Western culture. And why people who are not trained to be disciplined are ready to undertake the discipline of meditation. Somebody said to me the other day that the only discipline that is left in the West is dieting. For some other people there are physical workouts, jogging, and such. But people are also prepared today to follow a spiritual discipline like meditation—which asks them to meditate every day. To meditate in the morning before the day's work begins, and before we're caught up in the complexities and busyness of the day. And again, meditate in the early evening, at the end of the day's work—ideally, before the evening meal.

L.M.: We tend to become sleepy after a meal.

L.F.: Yes, it's always better to meditate before a meal. And don't leave meditation for late at night, until just before you go to sleep; because then you're quite likely, or more likely, to fall asleep.

L.M.: I guess that Father Bede Griffiths of Shantivanam ashram in India, who died in 1993, deserved a special dispensation. As he usually meditated in bed at night before going to sleep.

22

L.F.: At the age of eighty-six, I think he was able to do that.

L.M.: What part does the teacher of Christian meditation such as yourself have to play in the life of the individual Christian meditator? And what is the community's role?

L.F.: I feel quite strongly that the teacher—for the meditator in the Christian tradition—or for one who is coming to meditation in the Christian faith—that the teacher would be Christ. You have a living master in Christ. He is not just a Socrates or a Lao Tzu, who has left us beautiful words and ideas. The Christian believes that Christ is a living teacher. Christ is teaching us continuously, and moment by moment in the spirit—in the gift of the spirit. I think that this is the great reference point in Christian meditation, with regard to the teacher.

Saint Augustine says that Christ teaches us to pray. Because he prays in us—with us—and for us. That is significantly different from the Eastern tradition of the guru, where the guru is a very important figure. He or she who seems to the Westerner to be almost divinized. The Indians and the Tibetans tend to see the guru as the personification of the Absolute.

L.M.: Father Bede encountered that too.

L.F.: Yes, Father Bede did. I was with him once when one of the Hindu villagers came to his hut, and fell at his feet, and kissed his feet. Father Bede, who was the most humble person you could imagine, simply looked at me and smiled. And when the man had left he said: "You know, he's worshiping God in me, not me." So I think for the Christian that is the starting point.

It is also true to say of course that Christ teaches us through one another. And in the Christian church right from the very beginning—as Saint Paul makes clear in one of his letters. One of the most important ministries and ways of serving the community was to be a teacher. There are individuals who are called to teach. I don't think that their personality is the center of the teaching. But they are called to use whatever gifts they have to serve the community. They try to bring people to the experience of the teacher within—to Christ. The individual teacher in the Christian tradition always teaches within a community, whether small or large. Whether we see that as a monastic community, or a contemplative network like the World Community of Christian Meditation, or within the church as a whole. The Christian teacher never strikes out on his or her own—or on his or her own authority. The church clearly needs men and women of personal authority, but they always teach within the context of the community.

One of the ways you see that clearly in our community is all these small meditation groups that meet all around the world. In all sorts of places, every week a small group of people ranging from twenty to thirty at the very most; but usually, about ten or twelve people, will come together. There is a short teaching, or reading. And there is the meditation together—which is the most important reason for the gathering—and, some time for sharing. The leader of that group may simply play a tape, or give a talk, if they feel called to do that. But it is the community itself, the group itself, that becomes in a sense the medium for the presence of Christ, the teacher. The group performs the role of the teacher—though not exclusively.

L.M.: It certainly doesn't take the place of the individual's meditation in the morning and evening.

L.F.: No, certainly it doesn't do that. And it doesn't necessarily take the place of other individual teachers within the community. But in the Christian vision, the role of the teacher is in a way more subtle and more dimensional than in the East.

L.M.: It's more egalitarian in a sense. The teacher doesn't have a special aura or charisma. That's not required.

L.F.: You don't worship the teacher. You don't focus on, or get hung up on, the personality of the teacher. Though human dynamics are at work in any group, it can happen. As John Main used to say, the first job of the Christian teacher is to get out of the way as quickly as possible. And to let the spirit reveal itself, or herself, as the teacher.

L.M.: I find that when I'm sitting in meditation with a group, or in a Buddhist monastery, that my mind is usually calm and collected. But back at home, my meditation is often more jumbled and distracted.

L.F.: There is a great value in meditating together. Christians have always come together to pray. That is a very important aspect of Eastern traditions too. They call it *satsang*, or good company—the company of truth. We also have that idea of the church. We are enriched by the experience of meditating with others. And there are different dimensions to that experience. We have the simple, psychological encouragement of seeing other people remaining faithful to the same path as you are. When you are feeling discouraged, others can stimulate you to persevere. There is also the give and take of faith-sharing that is a very important part of deepening your dedication and perseverance.

And over and above that, there is the mysterious, sacramental quality to the group. Jesus said that when two or more are gathered in my name, there am I among them. The group itself forms a community—in the mystical sense, a real sense—the body of Christ. So I think that Christ is there in a sacramental way. That is why people often drive many miles on a cold winter's night, simply to sit for half an hour in silence with others. There is an experience of sacramental grace in the presence of the group.

L.M.: How can meditation be integrated into the whole of our lives, in this busy, rather confused social milieu? Whether it's in the area of friendship, love and marriage, or work?

L.F.: We are entering a new phase of the tradition—with the great expansion of contemplative practice among lay people and married people. That is going to change our whole theology of mysticism, for example. William Johnston in his book *Mystical Theology* says that the old language, which we used to describe the mystical life, the church, and mystical theology, is no longer adequate to describe the experience of married people, lay people, and those in other walks of life—who are following a contemplative path. In our community, I know many couples who meditate together every day; it is a very important quality in their marriage and in their family life. Many of them also share a ministry of teaching meditation to other people. There is a couple in their forties in Singapore. They're extremely busy; he is a busy financier, and his wife is busy with many things, raising a family. Yet they meditate together at home. And they have formed over the years about twenty or thirty meditation groups around the city that they coordinate.

L.M.: That's very impressive.

L.F.: It's a very important part of their life. And it's a real, spiritual ministry. So I think it's a new era now, when we have to take account of these realities. It is one of the most hopeful signs for the new form of the church that are slowly, painfully, laboriously appearing.

L.M.: Jesus has also said: by their fruits you shall know them. Do the fruits of meditation lead to a more loving, compassionate, and understanding view of things—with one's partner or business associate, among others? Maybe you've been doing some therapy, and it seems like you're experiencing a higher consciousness. Then somebody shouts at you and right away you lose your cool.

L.F.: You have to recognize that the fruits of this regular practice—integrated into your daily routine—are deep and powerful. Saint Paul calls them the harvest of the spirit: love, joy, peace, patience, kindness, goodness, fidelity, gentleness, and self-control. You find almost the same list of qualities in the Dhammapada, the Buddhist scripture. The fruits of meditation are undeniable.

L.M.: With this practice, the fruits of meditation are gradual. We're not to expect instant results.

L.F.: We shouldn't expect instant results. Although I do think you perceive a change beginning fairly immediately after you've made a commitment to meditation. I don't think that we should look for anything to happen in the meditation period itself; that is very important. There is a great deal of literature on meditation and spirituality, and on mystical experiences of other traditions on bookshelves today—that tends to give the impression that we meditate in order to gain extraordinary experiences during the meditation period. But in fact, if you look at the wisdom of all the great traditions, they insist that you don't look at meditation for results. If anything does happen, you basically ignore it and move on. That was the teaching of John of the Cross.

L.M.: And of *The Cloud* author.

L.F.: John Main says that if you have a particularly vivid vision in meditation, probably it would be more useful to attribute it to what you had for dinner. It is not so dramatic for many people. But the fruits do begin to appear in your personality and in your life. Somehow these changes that take place in you are reflected back to you through your relationships in the workplace, family life, and in intimate relationships. Suddenly you will notice that you are more patient, more loving, or a better listener. That will take you by surprise. Because we don't usually think of ourselves as having these qualities. We're never made proud by that discovery. Whereas you can be made proud if you are looking for extraordinary experiences.

L.M.: The spiritual ego gets inflated.

L.F.: One of the great warnings of the desert fathers to the monks was not to gain spiritual pride. That is a constant danger. Rather, when you do become aware of these fruits in you, you are humbled by it. You realize that this isn't your doing. This is the mainfestation of the divine life in you through your personality. That provokes a sense of wonder in us, rather than a sense of pride.

L.M.: I understand that you made a pilgrimage with other Christians to Bodh Gaya in India, which is the place of the Buddha's enlightenment. It seems that the way of meditation opens a door—or window—that enables us to learn from other religions.

L.F.: The dialogue between Christianity and the other religions is one of the great moments of the spirit in the modern world, and one of the great signs of hope. But it will only really be successful if we develop a dialogue at a level of silence too. We can realize that it is from our practicing meditation together that the most important changes take place. One of the problems of dialogue at the intellectual, philosphical level is that you either end up in conflict and banging the door, or you go for a kind of diplomatic resolution—you try to paper over, or ignore the differences. But when you have this common practice of meditation together in the dialogue process, then you come to the words and discussions and arguments, and sharing of viewpoints, in a very different way. You come with a certain detachment from the words. You are not idolizing the words, and absolutizing concepts.

L.M.: Saint John begins his Gospel by saying that, "in the beginning was the Word." Just what is that "word?" Does it mean the Bible, the Psalms? Yes, that is part of it. But isn't it also something else—that is, the creative action of the Holy Spirit, which we experience in meditation?

L.F.: Saint John spoke about the Word, the *Logos*, as in the beginning—and, as being God. He was using a Greek concept, the Logos; you also find the concept of the Word in the Hebrew Bible. The word of God that is coming to the prophets, and entering into the mind and consciousness of the prophets.

L.M.: Even through dreams, prophetic dreams.

L.F.: There is in the Greek idea of the Logos—which has been translated as reason and as speech—nuances that would not have been familiar to the Hebrew mind. The Logos goes back to the origins of Greek thought. As Heraclitus says, the Logos is the principle of harmony and order which affects, controls, or, guides—that is, I think, the word he uses—the whole universe. So you can see the attraction of that concept of the Logos to Saint John.

The Logos is a very important concept for Christians, as they enter into dialogue with other religions. Because we probably face—as Bede Griffiths liked to remind us—the same kind of challenge today in relation to non-Christian religions, as the early church faced in its encounter with the Gentile world.

We have to expand our terminology, our thinking; we have to allow other ways of expression and other ways of thought to become our own—as we struggle to speak about the inexpressible mystery of God. We can do that because we believe in the Logos. Because we believe that wherever human beings have discovered, or expressed truth, or beauty, or goodness, that has been through the Word of God. The Word has been present and is present in other religions. For us Christians, we believe that this Logos became flesh for the world; the Word became flesh in Jesus Christ. The fullness of the divinity was present in that unique individual in an unrepeatable way.

L.M.: Is there any ongoing dialogue between the Christian meditation community and the Islamic community? The Western media are almost overwhelmingly negative about Islam, and Muslims are largely associated with terrorists and dictators.

L.F.: I would like to have more dialogue with the Islamic world, and I have been personally involved in some cases, but not as much as I would like. There is this stereotyping of the Muslim world, and even of Muslim belief. There are some terrorists who blow up planes in the name of the Prophet

Mohammed; but if you look to the Koran, you see there is no justification for what they are doing.

L.M.: Also, some Christians probably think that Buddhists and Hindus are going to Hell.

L.F.: There is a great deal of prejudice and ignorance among a great many Western Christians toward other religions. I was giving a talk once and there was a well-educated, articulate, and intelligent person saying that Hindus were devil worshipers; and that to read their scriptures was very suspect and dangerous. We still do find a surprising amount of that kind of ignorance, which of course produces fear; and that produces hostility or even violence. It is a question of education, I think. Christian formation programs and religious education should include at least a sense of respect and reverence for other religions; and some of the basic elements of what they believe.

L.M.: What about children? They will be the adult generation of the future. Do you know of any educational approaches, perhaps in your schools in England, where children are being taught within a multifaith perspective that doesn't try to evangelize or convert; but, that really educates them about various religions?

L.F.: Many schools and educational systems do incorporate that into religious education. And students should receive that information about other religions in the context of their own tradition.

L.M.: It has to be rooted in one's own tradition.

L.F.: A lot of people are frightened about that approach today. Young parents will say: Well, I don't want to brainwash my children, I am going to let them make up their own minds. Yet, you wouldn't say: well, they are going to make up their mind about whether the earth goes around the sun—or, about Shakespeare. You expect children to be exposed to certain beliefs and opinions, and other traditions in a tolerant, respectful way. I personally think it is very important that there should be a teaching on meditation for children early on in school. Many of our meditators—those who are also teachers—have taught meditation to children—say, at the beginning of class for five minutes.

L.M.: Did the children enjoy the meditation?

L.F.: They enjoyed it immensely. Kids today are so bombarded with images, distractions, and entertainment. But they crave stillness and silence. Whenever I have meditated with young children or even with adolescents, it is like water being drunk up by thirsty ground.

L.M.: It is essential for the religions to get their own act together; and, in turn, do their share in helping the world get its act together—as far as global poverty, demilitarization, and world peace are concerned. How do you see Christianity's role in this dialogue with other religions?

L.F.: We have just come to the end of a long period of imperial, missionary Christianity where we were allied with great, imperial Western powers. And we went into Africa, Asia, and South America, bringing the Bible.

L.M.: Here in North America too.

L.F.: In North America too, of course—bringing in the Bible with the sword, and for economic advantage. Now, we're discovering a new kind of mission. There are many missionaries I know through our meditation community. They have a very strong sense of mission, but in a different sense—to realize the presence of Christ, and communicate the true teaching of Christ, the mystery of his humanity, and the depth of Christian faith. And, to be communicating that in a tolerant and humble way. Jesus tells us to wash one another's feet. Not to seek the first place at table. We have to hear those words, not only as individuals, but also as a church. It isn't our place as Christians to try to get to the top place at the table of the world religions. The true Christian would be very pleased to wash the feet of the other religions, and to serve unity, understanding, tolerance, and mutual respect. To be a servant, the person who comes in with the tea and coffee, rather than the one who is trying to control the agenda.

I was speaking with a Christian leader who is involved in inter religious dialogue at a very official level; I was shocked when I realized that for him it was all diplomacy and politics. It was getting the agenda right, and being very careful of your statements, and so on. What he seemed to me to miss was the sense that Christ is serving humanity through us. We don't have to be concerned about our diplomatic status; we don't have to try to win the argument. Sometimes, it is people who don't win the argument who are the most eloquent.

L.M.: I am reminded of how both Charles Foucauld and Carlo Carretto gave their authentic Christian witness among Islamic groups in North Africa, though they didn't attempt to convert them.

L.F.: A few years ago we got a letter from a French priest who had been in the Arctic for many years. He was coming to the end of his career and was about to retire. And he felt he was a complete failure. In all those years, he had maybe one or two baptisms. So he was looking at his life as something that may have been wasted. Then he began to meditate in the last year or so of his work there. And he realized through that dimension of prayer, that all those years he had been witnessing—he had been the presence of Christ to the people. That is really all we are called to do. We are not called to control the conversion process—that is between them and the Holy Spirit. Our work is to be, as fully as we can, channels of that humble love of Christ—that humble love which Christians need to tune into more.

L.M.: I noticed on the meditation community's website that you have what you call "bed and meditation," I think it is. So are people coming to your meditation centers the way they might go to a bed and breakfast place when traveling?

L.F.: Well, the "bed and med" as we call it was started by a wonderful couple in England, Daphne and Gordon Mackenzie. He recently died on a pilgrimage to the Holy Land. The idea was that this would be a way of developing community among meditators. We have a lot of people who would be happy to share their house, or room, on a bed and breakfast basis with other traveling meditators. They would meditate together, of course. And it has taken off; it is a very enriching, and economical, way of traveling.

L.M.: How does meditation help us to face—help us to cultivate—the good death—as Saint Paul said of himself: "I die daily"?

L.F.: John Main, shortly before his death, gave a series of teachings on death—on the role that meditation plays in preparing us for death. He was speaking within that great wisdom tradition that says: our life is very much a preparation for the way we die. Meditation trains us to die well. Because in meditation itself, we are entering into a death and resurrection process. For a Christian, this is the uniting of our own dying and rising with the central death and resurrection experience of Christ.

Every day has its own death: things we have to let go of. At certain crucial moments in our life, we may have to let go of people we would rather possess or control. We may have to let go of images of ourselves; we may have to let go of status and material wealth we have gotten used to. And letting go of these things is dying. I think when you are meditating every day, you are able to face those little deaths more peacefully. They still hurt. Nobody wants to die. You may still put up a fight. But meditation grounds you in the life of the spirit. And that grounding in the life of God gives you the confidence to look death in the eye. And to accept it as part of life.

That is why meditation reduces the fear of death. I don't say that it takes away the fear of death altogether. Because the fear of death is inherent in us, deeply. But it certainly reduces the fear of death, and prevents us from becoming a neurotic about death. Because we learn that every time we go into death with faith—always, always, and always—there is new life. We learn that on the pulsebeat of our own experience. Meditation highlights that and makes us conscious of that at a very deep level. And from that deep level, we are able to recognize the meaning of death on the ordinary physical and material levels as well.

We learn that death is not the end of life. It is a point of transformation.

INTEGRAL YOGA WITH SWAMI SATCHIDANANDA

L.M.: What are the key teachings of Integral Yoga meditation?

S. SATCH: Meditation aims to help you have, to help you get a grip, over your own mind. It begins with the body—by way of doing some yoga postures, you gain control over the bodily actions and bodily functions. From there you go on to the vital body, the breathing. You learn how to get a grip over the breath.

L.M.: The *prana*.

S. SATCH: *Pranayama*—so there is slow, regular, deep breathing—and then, a little control. There are different types of pranayama.

L.M.: It's not an exaggerated breathing, or straining.

S. SATCH: No, no, none of these practices should be done with any strain. They should be done up to one's capacity; gradually, gently, with no forcing.

L.M.: Or, our minds might rebel.

S. SATCH: Yes, yes, and next is controlling the senses—the body, the breath, the senses. And of course, controlling the mind: the mind works through the senses. You control the senses one by one, and through that process you control the mind. So then, how do you take care of your sight, your speech, your sense of smell and hearing, all the senses? You don't have to simply follow the senses wherever they lead you. Instead, you should demand that the senses do whatever you want. Suppose the eye says, I want to go see a movie. And you say, no, I have to go to church. Who wins ultimately? If you win, then you have control over your eyes; and if the eyes win, you lose control over them. The habit of eating is also like that. You have nice sumptuous food, and after the meal somebody brings you a delicious cake. So you feel like eating it.

L.M.: Definitely, we do.

S. SATCH: But you say to your mind: no, you have eaten so much good food, you can have it later. But the mind says: I want it now. If you succumb to that, you are not in control of your mind—through your tongue.

L.M.: So it is a disciplining.

S. SATCH: It is disciplining the senses. Then comes the practice of meditation itself—that begins with concentration. As soon as you try to control your mind, it doesn't want to stay one way, in one place. It will run here and there. You will think of something, and within a few seconds, it will go somewhere else. You think of a rose, you admire the rose and how beautiful it is. But immediately, your mind will jump to somebody who gave you the rose a few days back; then you will think of him instead of the rose. You think: Where did I meet him? Your mind roams around, all over. Then you realize that I started with the rose, but now the mind is running away. Bring it back to the rose. That is, you fix or focus on a certain point. The mind runs here and there; and you bring it back to the point again and again. That is concentration—or *dharana*—according to the Yoga system.

34

L.M.: Is a mantra employed in the meditation?

S. SATCH: Yes, at that time we also give a mantra so that the mind has something to hold onto; and you keep repeating that mantra.

L.M.: Continuosly, even if you don't have any distractions?

S. SATCH: In the beginning you forcefully try to repeat it, continuously. And then gradually, the mind will repeat by itself without even your awareness of that.

L.M.: Automatically?

S. SATCH: Automatically—so that one part of the mind is always with the mantra; even though you allow the mind to do various things.

L.M.: The so-called worldly, external activities.

S. SATCH: Yes, you do some activities, but part of the mind will always be there on the mantra. When you finish a job outside, you go back to the mantra; then another work comes along and you take part of the mind to the other job. So the mantra remains constantly in the mind. That way you slowly begin to tame the mind to stay in one place.

L.M.: It seems to be a very slow and gradual process for most of us.

S. SATCH: When the concentration becomes firm, then you begin to meditate. It is at that point that your practice is called meditation.

L.M.: And before that?

S. SATCH: Nobody meditates right away. The mind runs around, and slowly you bring it back, back, back again. And then you begin to meditate. Then the mind will be there, at least for half an hour, or fifteen, or ten minutes. Then you have gained some mastery over your own mind.

L.M.: I know that with my own meditation practice, even after many years the mind still runs out.

35

S. SATCH: Yes, yes, yes.

L.M.: But one shouldn't be discouraged. What if the mind is very active and scattered?

S. SATCH: Again, it depends also on your day-to-day activities, how involved you are—how much you are attached to your activities. If the mind is attached to them, it will not stay put in your meditation. You have to reduce the attachments in the outside world, though you don't have to be completely detached. If your outside activities are being performed for personal reasons, then the attachment is more.

L.M.: We need to reattach the mind inwardly.

S. SATCH: Yes, inwardly—and also, outward activities—mostly, you should do them for the sake of others. That is a selfless action, which we call *karma yoga*. Karma is what you do for your own sake; you don't worry about others.

L.M.: Selfishly, acting selfishly.

S. SATCH: You put yourself first. Karma yoga is putting others first.

L.M.: That's what Lord Krishna means in the Bhagavad Gita in his teachings on karma yoga.

S. SATCH: Yes, karma yoga—when your entire life is built on serving others, your mind is under control. It is selfishness that disturbs the mind.

L.M.: A very good point. Meditation—concentration leading to meditation—is the cultivating of that unselfishness, that self-lessness.

S. SATCH: Apart from the practice of meditation, your day-to-day life should be regulated like that: making sure that you do everything as a service to others.

L.M.: There is also a kind of atmosphere of meditation and service we could develop in the larger part of the day when we are not meditating.

S. SATCH: Whatever you do becomes a meditation then. There is a beautiful saying in the Bhagavad Gita which says: whatever you do, whether you eat something, you do something, you sleep, or you offer something to others, or you pray—whatever you do, do it in the name of God; for others' sake, not for yourself. Then everything becomes meditation. Meditation need not be only when you go and sit in a corner and repeat a mantra. When you do a thing, do that one thing at a time. When you sleep, you sleep; don't think of tomorrow's activities. When you eat, you eat; don't think of your business. That's why I don't like these business lunches.

L.M.: I don't like them either.

S. SATCH: They invite you to have lunch, but talk about business. Are you eating, or talking there? So one thing at a time, and that too, well done. That you could call meditation.

L.M: Being present, really mindful.

S. SATCH: Be mindful of anything you do.

L.M.: That would also perhaps develop better qualities in meditation?

S. SATCH: Sure, sure, even your daily life will be successful in whatever you do, because you're applying the entire mind on it. When you apply your whole mind on something, you will certainly achieve success.

L.M.: What about the role of the teacher on the spiritual path? You are a teacher or guru. And in various scriptures, we have Lord Krishna, we have Jesus; also the Buddha and Guru Nanak, among others. How can we better understand the role of the guru—one which is so often misunderstood—especially here in the West, in America?

S. SATCH: The role of the teacher is that he should not think that he is a teacher. He is not a teacher; he is living a life and others watch and learn from that. By setting an example, living what you want others to live. But no teacher is complete, because the teacher himself or herself will still be learning.

37

L.M.: The teacher then is always learning, and not only the disciples or students.

S. SATCH: Yes, and more than the teacher's words, the life itself—and the way you conduct yourself—should educate them. That is what Krishna did. Whatever he did, he did mindfully. He didn't hesitate to do any kind of work; he was a charioteer. He washed his horses, cleaned the chariot, ran the chariot. At the same time, he advised Arjuna. Krishna was working on different levels, at different positions. Whatever he did, he did it well, without feeling any inferiority or superiority about that.

L.M.: Some disciples choose to adulate the teacher, the guru. They are all but saying, I don't really have to meditate. The guru will save me in the end. Is that realistic?

S. SATCH: No, no, you have to save yourself. The teacher will only guide you. It is almost like a highway; the signpost says: Washington—200 miles. You don't go and worship the signpost. Rather, you go in the right direction for two hundred miles; then only you will reach Washington. The teacher can show you the way, he cannot take you there. You have to follow through. If somebody can take you there easily, it makes things easy for you. God could do that; God loves everybody, we say. Why can't God do that? God also sometimes allows you to make mistakes; and by your own mistakes, that makes you learn.

L.M.: We have to pick ourselves up again.

S. SATCH: So take the teacher's advice, and keep and follow the teachings. The teacher is nothing but the teaching; the teaching is the important thing. People adore and worship the teacher, but forget the teaching. What good is it then? It is almost like worshiping a book without knowing what it says inside.

L.M.: I saw that worship of the book at the Golden Temple, the holiest shrine of the Sikhs, in India. I got the impression that the Sikhs had forgotten the essence of the teachings of their founder Guru Nanak.

S. SATCH: Many religions worship the book. Jewish people revere the Torah, but how many people follow what the Torah says? Hindus worship the Bhagavad Gita and even build temples for the book, but they don't know one verse.

L.M.: They're not living those truths of the scriptures.

S. SATCH: Mere worshiping of the ladder will not make it go up.

L.M.: The book, or the teacher.

S. SATCH: It's just a ladder. You say: "Oh, this is the ladder my teacher gave me. I worship it, I adore it. How can I step on it?" Because it's a holy object, no. Then what is the point of giving a ladder to you?

L.M.: The teaching is there to be used.

S. SATCH: You have to go up; and once you reach the top, you go on your way and leave the ladder for somebody else. You don't keep on holding onto the ladder saying: this is the ladder that brought me up.

L.M.: We learn to let go.

S. SATCH: Let go—you even have to let go of the teacher himself.

L.M.: That can be difficult, since a certain devotion to the teacher is also necessary.

S. SATCH: In the beginning, it is necessary. After some time however, even that should be discarded, renounced. Because you're attached then to that form.

L.M.: The teacher's outer form and personality. Does the teacher also have an inner form—the true, eternal form in God?

S. SATCH: Yes, yes.

L.M.: We shouldn't get caught up in the external.

S. SATCH: The external will not always be there; we may miss seeing that one day. Does it mean that when the teacher is gone, the teaching is also gone?

L.M.: There is also the path of discipleship. I see here at Yogaville both *sannyasis*, or renunciates, and singles and married householders.

S. SATCH: Yes, both of those paths are good, all are following the same teaching.

L.M.: One is not higher or lower than the other.

S. SATCH: No, no, some have dedicated their lives to public service; and some serve their family and the public. There is no reason to differentiate between them. Even sannyasis need householders: otherwise, where will they get their food; where will they go begging? Lord Buddha says the bhikkus should go for alms, as they're not cooking food at the monastery. So if there are no householders, who will feed them?

L.M: All the monks and nuns would die out if there weren't any more families.

S. SATCH: That's right, everybody is doing their part. All are equal servants. For example, Krishna was a householder.

L.M: Arjuna, too.

S. SATCH: Arjuna was—there's nothing wrong in being a householder. Many teachers were householders. But they were not "hold" in the house—that is the main thing. Householders are serving the immediate family; and in their spare time, they are serving the outer family. Their immediate family is only given into their care; they are the custodians, the trustees of their family. Not my family, my wife, my children. No, the Lord has given you all of these people to support, to take care of them. You are only a baby sitter.

L.M.: Here at Yogaville, a balance has been struck. It's a good example of community.

S. SATCH: Sannyasis are here, singles are here, married people are here. We respect everybody, and everybody has a job to do.

L.M.: Being a householder doesn't mean one is held back from complete liberation.

S. SATCH: Mentally, you are not attached to things, personal attachments are not there. It doesn't matter where you are. Your main thing in life is to serve, whether you are a sannyasi, or a householder, or a single person. It's service, it's all service.

L.M.: Meditation and service are both so important. What can we do about the negative qualities in us, the moods and actions that the mind generates? Specifically, those attributes of the mind that get in the way of selfless service—anger, for one.

S. SATCH: Those are all based on selfishness. You are angry because you didn't personally get what you want. Selfishness comes in there; normally, all these negative qualities will be there. Slowly, we develop the opposite of them.

L.M.: We should cultivate the virtues.

S. SATCH: Develop the virtues, as opposed to the vices. Patanjali says, in his Yoga Sutra: when you have a feeling of hatred, develop love for that person. You force it; forcefully you say, I love him, I love him.

L.M.: At the start, it's almost like acting.

S. SATCH: I call it a lube job.

L.M.: A lube job?

S. SATCH: You know, for the car. When you take your car for a lubrication, the grease is old. How do they eliminate the old grease and put in new grease? Simply, they inject the new grease; automatically, the old grease is pushed out. So if you inject the virtue, the vice will be pushed out. But the injection should be powerful and forceful in the beginning.

L.M.: It has to be a daily habit.

S. SATCH: Be aware of your problems. And cultivate the opposite qualities. At the same time, ask yourself: Why am I angry? What is the cause? You will then come down ultimately to: that I didn't get what I want. I found him or her interfering in what I want. So you get angry, you hate them. You make them your enemy.

L.M.: We should be making friends of them, converting our enemies into friends.

S. SATCH: Think of the negative aspects of it. If you're angry, then you are affecting yourself.

L.M.: The body—our bodies.

S. SATCH: Body suffers, mind suffers. You get stressed. So you are affecting yourself even before you affect the other person. It's not worth it. So we should also practice self-analysis.

L.M.: What does living the good life really mean, as the path of Integral Yoga understands it to be?

S. SATCH: What is the good life? I use three words for that, they summarize the entire yoga, or entire religion—all religions. The first word is easeful.

L.M.: Easeful.

S. SATCH: Easeful, not to be dis-easeful. To be easeful is to be peaceful. And then, by being easeful and peaceful, you become useful.

L.M.: Before that, we're not useful.

S. SATCH: No, we will be a problematic person. If you're not peaceful and easeful, you'll be a nuisance to others.

L.M.: Even to yourself.

S. SATCH: So protect, take care of your health and peace of mind. Then you are fit to serve others. Then you could become a useful person. Then, it is a good living. Make sure that you are always happy and peaceful. Don't do anything that will make you unhappy, and that will disturb your peace or your ease. Disease is nothing but disturbed ease; you had ease before, but you disturbed it. Find out what disturbed your ease. Stay away from those things: my wrong thinking, my wrong food, my wrong activity. You maintain your ease and peace, and then people will find a use for you.

L.M.: One of the greatest fears which meditation seeks to overcome is the fear of death. The ego fears to die.

S. SATCH: Understand what death means—that is the only way to get beyond the fear. What is death after all—who dies? Everybody says: he died. We normally talk like that: Oh, he's dead and gone. Analyze that sentence: dead and gone. It means the body is dead, so he is gone. He was using the body, but now it can't be used any more. Either he became old, or something else, so he left the body. He didn't die, probably he got a better body, another one. If your car is not useful anymore, what do you do? You junk it, get a new model. That's what death means.

L.M.: The problem is that unless the consciousness is developed, the inner consciousness, we are much more attached to our body than say, our car.

S. SATCH: That's the problem, though people are also attached to their cars.

L.M.: That's true, absolutely.

S. SATCH: I heard that one cinema star in Los Angeles buried herself with her Ferrari.

L.M.: That's a pretty big plot.

S. SATCH: She was attached to that car, and anything you are attached to, you carry a burden. So you use it, but don't attach it—don't get attached to it. You take good care of it, you use it for sometime; and then anything that is created will decompose.

43

L.M.: It's natural.

S. SATCH: Nobody is physically permanent. We all have to leave the body one day or another. It doesn't matter if I leave the body, I'm going to get a new one. If you think that way, you will be happy to die. Having an old body, and living with pills, and all that.

L.M.: It's not much fun.

S. SATCH: Magnesium, calcium—it's not much fun.

L.M.: Is there some way, say through meditation, that we don't have to be reborn, or reincarnate, into a human body?

S. SATCH: We don't have to. Why do we get the body, first of all? We want to travel somewhere, we get a car. If we don't want to travel anywhere, do we then want a car?

L.M.: It's not necessary.

S. SATCH: If the mind doesn't want to enjoy anything anymore; and the mind is satisfied, it has no desires—there is no need for a body. That is what you call *nirvana*, desirelessness. Buddha taught about nirvana; nirvana means nakedness. The mind is completely naked. It doesn't want, it doesn't hold onto anything—not even a single desire. So there is nothing left to be fulfilled; if you want to fulfill a desire, then you need a body. All our desires can only be fulfilled through our bodies. Think of a desire which you can fulfill without the body.

L.M.: It's impossible.

S. SATCH: Impossible—you eat something, you need a tongue and mouth; you smell something, you need a nose; you see something, you need eyes; you want to think, you have to have a brain. But when the time comes that you don't want to do anything, you don't need the body anymore. You are liberated.

L.M.: At that point your love is perfected, your love for all beings. Can you now serve in other nonphysical realms?

44

S. SATCH: You don't even serve. Rather, others make you serve. You don't even feel like serving then; even that desire is not there. You say, I want to serve people; it's a desire, it requires a body. But you are then without any desire. The sun doesn't think: I'm giving light to everybody. The sun is there, that's all. Can you say that the sun gives light?

L.M.: No, it is light.

S. SATCH: It is light. That is what the liberated state is: I am that I am—that's all.

L.M.: What about the need for a sense of humor to cope with life's myriad ups and downs, the adversity, negativity, and suffering in life?

S. SATCH: Just have fun, just have fun. You enjoy everything, you think of everything as having fun. Good things, bad things, adversities, it doesn't matter—it's all fun. Even when you go to a movie, you don't always watch nice things.

L.M.: No, sometimes we don't.

S. SATCH: If it's all nice, nobody will watch that movie.

L.M.: We need something more dramatic.

S. SATCH: You can't have a movie with only heroes and heroines; you should also have villains. Without a villain, no movie is charming, interesting. So life is like that. We can enjoy both—the ups and the downs. I call it being a surfer. If you want to surf, don't look for a flat sheet of water.

L.M.: You need crashing waves.

S. SATCH: Big waves—the bigger the wave, the more is your enjoyment. Waves means the ups and downs, that you enjoy the ups and downs in life. That's what fun means. You're supposed to always have fun, fun, and more fun, in life. Nothing but fun. I could even say that you are the product of fun.

L.M.: I hope so.

S. SATCH: Papa and mama had some fun, and you are here now. You are born of fun, you are a product of fun; you are living fun—and your going out, your dying, is also fun. Everything is fun. That is what we call *lila* in the Hindu language, in India.

L.M.: That is the divine play.

S. SATCH: Divine play, the *krishna lila*—*lila* means play.

L.M.: So then we accept our role in the play, we stop resisting our path, our life.

S. SATCH: That's right, the whole world is a dramatic stage. We are all taking parts on that stage; we are all pawns in the hands of that puppeteer.

L.M.: Yet on the meditative path, on the yoga path, do we have a responsibility to reduce the suffering we see around us; or at least, not add to others' suffering?

S. SATCH: When you see others as others, and their suffering as their suffering, you are not seeing the ultimate goal. You have descended to a different level, the level of duality. And on that level, certainly you can do whatever you want, you can alleviate their suffering—that is your duty. But on the primary, nondualistic level, we have no duty. You are not doing anything, you are a puppet, you are made to do things.

L.M.: By God?

S. SATCH: By God, or by the ultimate reality. So let "that" use you in anyway it needs. "Make me a humble instrument," Saint Francis prays. An instrument doesn't demand. The tape recorder didn't demand of you: "Record swami's life." You could have recorded some rock and roll. Whatever you record, it doesn't bother the tape recorder. It's neutral. Everything is like that in nature. Is fire good or bad? Use it to cook food, it is good; use it to set fire to your house, it's bad. Is fire responsible for that?

L.M.: Not at all.

S. SATCH: So if you are an instrument, you are not responsible for anything. You are made to do that; you are doing it, that's all. This feeling of "doership," of being the doer, is also not there.

L.M.: At that stage one doesn't think: I did it. Yet don't I want to be applauded for my good deed?

S. SATCH: When you think that you are doing it, then you are responsible. It's your work then, and you have to face the consequences.

L.M.: The karmic consequences?

S. SATCH: Yes, the karmic.

L.M.: If we don't want to be bound by that karmic law, we have to—the ego has to surrender?

S. SATCH: Surrender to God, just like Arjuna said: Lord, I don't know anything, you tell me what to do, I do it. In the beginning, he argued with Krishna about not having, not wanting, to fight. But ultimately he realized his foolishness and said: I surrender to you, you make me do anything you want.

L.M.: Arjuna had to take the warrior's path, the path of action.

S. SATCH: Krishna could have won the war without Arjuna, without any army. With a single finger, he could have done everything. But he was using them. The heart of karma yoga is depicted in the Bhagavad Gita. The very title *Gita* itself tells you: *gi-ta*, or *ta-gi*. *Tagi* means to renounce or dedicate; so *Gita* becomes *tagi*.

L.M.: So renounce and one has everything?

S. SATCH: Renounce even the feeling that you are doing things. I am not the doer, I am not the enjoyer, I am just an instrument.

L.M.: In your experience, by taking the broadest, most expansive definition of what meditation is—is that the best approach to take?

S. SATCH: It begins in a small way; it becomes broader later on.

L.M.: The initial focus has to be simple.

S. SATCH: It starts off simple. You go there, you sit there and repeat your mantra for a certain number of times a day. Certain *molas*, you count your molas; in the beginning, there are all these restrictions. Slowly, slowly, slowy, all these little restrictions will be gone. Your life becomes a meditation then.

L.M.: The mola is similar to the Christian rosary.

S. SATCH: Yes—in the beginning, you are conscious of all those things. It's like anything. You practice the piano, and at first you are very conscious of the keys, of your fingers. Then after a long time, you don't even see them.

L.M.: Your own life and teachings wonderfully embody the ongoing spirit of dialogue among the world religions and spiritual traditions. What do you think we still need to do together now to enter into real communion with one another? Your writings indicate that you are optimistic about the coming of a new spiritual age. So how do we bring about more dialogue and harmony— and even the kingdom of God on earth?

S. SATCH: In your own way, begin in your own circle first.

L.M.: Where you, we, are living?

S. SATCH: Where you are living, in what you are doing. Bring that harmony there, and slowly let it expand. Charity begins at home—we don't have to go looking somewhere else.

L.M.: We don't have to move to Yogaville.

S. SATCH: No, no, you set a good example, say Yogaville—that it is model for others to see. Then it gets expanded, as others see this and think: why can't we also do that?

L.M.: Right where we are.

S. SATCH: That's why I started the ecumenical worship service together with various clergymen some thirty years ago. And it started going—now, everybody, everywhere is doing it—no gathering is performed without having the ecumenical service. There is always some Christian clergy, Jewish rabbis, and Hindu monks together—so it slowly, slowly expanded.

L.M.: When was the first ecumenical service held?

S. SATCH: In the summer of 1953, in Sri Lanka.

L.M.: Why did you start it?

S. SATCH: We started on Guru Poorima Day, which is the full moon day in July—Guru Poorima is dedicated to the worship of one's own master. We were planning for the worship service, but I noticed that all of my friends are Christians, Muslims, Buddhists, Hindus. Here I am as a Hindu, worshiping my guru, Swami Sivananda. But all these other people are helping me, and how would they feel?

L.M.: Would they feel included?

S. SATCH: So I thought, why not put up and show pictures of all the gurus and worship together? They were excited over that idea; and immediately, they brought thirty or forty pictures to put all over the platform. And then, we celebrated that day as an ecumenical service.

L.M.: That was the very first one.

S. SATCH: In 1953—and immediately, everybody wanted to do it; every month they started doing that all over Sri Lanka.

L.M.: You had not done it in India before this?

S. SATCH: No—and then I came to America in 1966, where I was surrounded by Christian monks, rabbis, Zen monks, and everybody. So we all wanted to have some interfaith gathering. In the beginning, we all began talking about our religions and the commonalities in our religions. Just talking.

L.M.: So you began a dialogue.

S. SATCH: And at one of our retreats we said: We are talking, talking, talking—why not do something? So let's do some worship service together. We all appreciate light as a symbol; nobody objects to that. If I were to put only Shiva, Buddha, or Krishna, you Christians will object; or Jesus, Hindus will object.

L.M.: How true.

S. SATCH: But if I use a light, all will enjoy it. So let's put a light in the middle of a table; and sit around and worship that light, each in our own way.

L.M.: No one way, but each individual.

S. SATCH: Everybody makes his own way according to their own tradition. The object is the same, but the forms of worship are different. Then, every retreat and gathering commenced with the ecumenical service. We call it Yoga Ecumenical Service—YES.

L.M.: Yes.

S. SATCH: We say yes to everything. That went on for several years. Then one day day I thought, we are doing it here and there. Why not a permanent place for it? That's when I started thinking about LOTUS.

L.M.: The Light of Truth Universal Shrine here at Yogaville.

S. SATCH: You've seen LOTUS? In the middle there is one light. It goes up, and then spirals out. It represents the one and same light that gives light to all the religions.

L.M.: Even though LOTUS and indeed all at Yogaville positively anticipate and proclaim the hope of universal brotherhood and the kingdom of God, when we look at the daily news it's mostly bad news.

S. SATCH: The newspaper publishes bad news—it is unwashed news. The good news, nobody reads it. If people read good news more, they will print good news. But if they print only good news, newspapers will go broke. On the other hand, newspapers could educate the public to read more good things. There is a Tamil saying in India that "a woman can make or break." I twist that to, "a pen can make or break." We were once at a United Nations gathering with some media people. I told them that the pen makes or breaks, because you are writing the headlines of the day for the world. What are people reading about, good things or bad things? I told them, you are making people think of bad things; and the more they read that, they become bad. They send out bad vibrations. Look at poor President Clinton. He did nothing more than what other presidents have done; JFK did more. But at that time, the media didn't write about such things. Now they are writing, and it's a big explosion.

L.M.: It is a real problem.

S. SATCH: I went and opened the Woodstock Festival.

L.M.: You said an opening prayer there in 1969?

S. SATCH: All the newspapers wrote nasty things about all the rubbish and about how people smoked marijuana and danced naked. But none of them wrote about the nice, positive things. For three days and nights in the rain, hundreds of thousands of people lived together without any friction or any violence. But the media didn't appreciate that. So I told them at the UN: You are like vultures or eagles—eagles fly high, but do you know where their eyes are looking? Where the dead bodies are. We don't see the good things, we only see the bad things. So newspaper people, the media, should change their attitude and start writing more about good things.

L.M.: You're right. The vision for the coming spiritual age or renaissance is to be able to bring about a better world, through meditation and service to others that we have been talking about. We need to see the best in everyone as Saint Francis did.

S. SATCH: In everything you have good and bad, it's a mixture. But when you see the good things, and develop that, and improve and encourage that,

that will also encourage public opinion. People should think about good things; they shouldn't think about only bad things. Even though, they are there. I don't say that things are all clean, all good. But, ignore that—take and appreciate the good things that are there. That will encourage them to see and do good things.

L.M.: It's our attitude of mind.

S. SATCH: In a hospital, you go to see the patients. Some people go there and say: You look so terrible, what is wrong with you? Within a few days, the patient will die. If instead you say to them: Oh, you look all right, much better than yesterday; the doctor must be treating you well—I think you're taking a good medicine. Encourage them, they'll get well and come out of the bed; give them confidence and courage.

See good in everything, see good in everything.

BON DZOGCHEN WITH TENZIN WANGYAL RINPOCHE

L.M.: What is Bon meditation? And especially, what is the essence of Bon Dzogchen practice?

T.W.: First of all, I think it is important to know what Bon is. Bon is the indigenous tradition of Tibet. Within the tradition, it is believed to have begun about 17,000 years ago in central Asia; and from there, it eventually came to be introduced into the western and central parts of Tibet. The founder of Bon religion is known as Tonpa, or the Lord, Shenrab Miwo. Basically, Bon teachings contain all the sutra teachings, tantra teachings, and Dzogchen teachings. I always say that the Bon religion is very unique, because it contains—and ranges from—the raw, elemental shamanic teachings to the very high teachings of Dzogchen, which is the teaching of illumination, of light. And also it has, between them, all the energy aspects of healing. So there is a very wide range of teachings that Bon contains. The shamanistic teachings of Bon are very much working with the raw elements; and it is very, very similar to the indigenous traditions around the world.

L.M.: Such as the Native American.

T.W.: Such as the Native Americans have; also that are in Peru and in other parts of the world. It is working with raw elements—working with fire is like the sweat lodge; and working with smokes, fumigations, purifications; and with prayerflags. A great amount of respect is paid to nature, to mother earth: to trees, rocks, and the mountains. Indigenous peoples don't just regard them as a place or thing which we own. Instead, they consider them to be another entity—a being there which is living with them. We have to live in harmony with them.

On the other hand, now there is so much environmental destruction and pollution that causes new, or newly appearing, diseases. Indigenous traditions believe in this way. In Tibet they call it "time disease." There are Tibetan prophecies which say that, in the future, there will be a lot of new diseases which you don't even know the names of. They are caused by environmental destructions and pollution. They, indigenous peoples, believe this. And so, the respect paid to nature is very, very similar in all these traditions.

L.M.: It's sacred then, nature is sacred.

T.W.: Nature is very sacred. In the technologically developed countries like America, of course there are also a lot of benefits in such developments. We discover many means of curing disease. So there are many, many benefits too.

L.M.: Yes, there are.

T.W.: But at the same time, with all this development, it loses something of the spirit in nature and humanity. For example, many people don't even know how to relate to themselves. They see other people as matter, as things; rather, than as really human beings. Sometimes they don't see themselves as a being, as a human being.

L.M.: Their thinking works in a mechanical way, they see others more as objects to use.

T.W.: More as objects—you know, if the computer doesn't work, they don't know how to think. They depend on it; everything stops if the computer stops.

Dzogchen teachings, and specifically Dzogchen teachings within Bon, have very much to do with discovering the nature of mind in onself. There is a line in Dzogchen teachings where we say: self-arising wisdom is the base; all the negative emotions are manifested energy; seeing emotions as mistaken is an error; leaving them as they are—letting emotions be in their nature—is the method; and, going beyond hope and fear is the result. This is a summary of what Dzogchen teachings are. As things are means: we don't know how to see anymore—how to see the way things really are. Neither in ourself, nor in other things, nor with what we perceive in the world. We are always so dualistic and confusion-filtered in our mind, our whole senses, our eyes—our vision.

We cannot see things as things are. We say, I see this cup. But I don't just see a cup. I see my cup—I see it is not your cup—I see this need to protect it; and I see so many things which do not belong to the cup. All those dualistic aspects of oneself we reflect in the outside world. This obscures the nature of mind; all this obscures oneself—it obscures nature, also.

So then, Dzogchen is the way of overcoming one's own dualistic obscurations; and of discovering the wisdom inside oneself. In Tibet, Dzogchen teachings are mainly practiced in the Bon tradition; and in the Nyingma school— the early Tibetan Buddhist tradition; these are the two main schools that practice Dzogchen. In some ways, Dzogchen is very similar to Zen Buddhism, and to Chan in China. Though there are some differences between Zen and Dzogchen as well—in Zen, there is a very strong emphasis on sunyata.

L.M.: Emptiness.

T.W.: Emptiness—and, the aspect of working with what in Bon is called clarity is much less. In Dzogchen teaching, there is the inseparable quality of clarity and emptiness. This dual emphasis is very strong on the base level; and on the path level, it is also very different. With Zen practice, people sit for a long time; sitting practice is the main practice.

L.M.: They have very long sittings.

T.W.: Yes, Zen sitting means sitting in sunyata—reflecting on emptiness. Dzogchen practitioners perform all kinds of energy work, and practices in their meditation sittings; this energy work is also an aspect of clarity. Also, Dzogchen will include the practices of the *dark retreat*—of *sun-gazing* and *sky-gazing*. All these vision-oriented, visual practices are done in relation to emptiness; but, in Zen, they are not done. Those are the differences at the path level.

There are also differences between Zen and Bon at the result level. In Dzogchen, there is a lot of practice of what we call the *rainbow body*; a lot of practitioners have achieved the body of light, or the rainbow body. But in Zen, that too is not a concept, or practice there.

L.M.: Is that a full liberation when you have reached the rainbow body?

T.W.: Yes—though that is not to say that Zen is not a way of complete liberation, also. But the method of achievement is very different. So in Bon, there is the clarity aspect on the base level; there are practices of light on the path level; and the achievement of the rainbow body is on the result level. These are the distinctive aspects—and differences with Zen practice—in the base, and the path, and the result levels, in Bon.

L.M.: What exactly does Bon mean by the terms emptiness and clarity?

T.W.: Bon—the word *Bon*—means nature; it means existence. It means recitation, reciting—it means many different things. In general, Bon means the indigenous religion of Tibet.

L.M.: How would you do, how does someone do the sky-gazing practice, for instance?

T.W.: Well, first one would have to do a lot of preliminary practices, preparatory practices, in order to do that. One would have to develop a lot of concentration ability. Then once you want to focus on one thing, the mind remains there. For example, people want to stay in one place. Yet when they move to a place, soon they again want to find another place to be. Their mind can never be, or stay, in one place. This means they don't have concentration of the mind.

L.M.: The mind is always moving.

56

T.W.: It's always moving. But the moving is not under their control; they are driven by their mind.

L.M.: Yes, we are.

T.W.: So developing a great deal of concentration is necessary. Then on the basis of having achieved concentration, we develop something called contemplation. Contemplation is discovering the truth, the wisdom in onself. That is called contemplation, or *rigpa*. Once you discover that, and stabilize or maintain that, then you go on to the visionary practices—such as dark retreat, sky-gazing, sun-gazing. Bon says that the mind is like a waterfall: it is constantly moving. As you practice more, it stabilizes a little bit more. It—the mind—comes down, as water will get to the ground; it moves one way. Then, another level of movement will be like a hawk that is flying in one place. It is not moving in different directions; it is only moving in one place. And then, the next level is like a turtle in a vase.

L.M.: Like the turtle.

T.W.: When the turtle puts in its face, it doesn't move; it takes all its hands and legs, and just stays there.

L.M.: In its shell.

T.W.: In its shell—it is still, not moving. The final level is like a clear sky, when all the clouds dissolve into space; the mind becomes like a clear sky. There is no movement—there is no substance, or duality, either.

L.M.: Do the meditation practices for beginner level students of Bon vary for different students?

T.W.: No, they are general practices as I said. You develop concentration; then you develop contemplation; and then you stabilize the mind through visionary practices.

L.M.: That could all take many years.

T.W.: Many, many years.

L.M.: What are the different benefits of lay and monastic discipleship in Bon? Some people might think: well, I will only reach enlightenment or liberation if I leave the world completely and become a monk or nun. That kind of thinking has been encouraged in Christian—and perhaps, Buddhist—monasticism for over a thousand years.

T.W.: Well, from the point of view of a monastery, of monks, there is a very strong Bon tradition of monastery disciplines. Maybe their point of view will be very much like that. But that is not necessarily true. You are a monk: you have to eat, right?

L.M.: Indeed, we all have to.

T.W.: You have to sleep, and wear warm clothes when it is cold; or take off your warm clothes when it is hot. You are dependent on the raw elements—as lay people are dependent on them. But mainly, the principle of monkhood is that somehow you are trying to arrange and control the disturbances of the mind, which you are trying to avoid—such as not killing; not having male and female relationships, and sexual intercourse. We know that even in the lay community, relationships are one of the hardest things to deal with.

L.M.: Especially, these days.

T.W.: Today, especially; so it make sense for monks to think: Oh, that is one of the hardest things—better not to deal with that right from the beginning. But on the other hand, not everybody's decision is made like that. Perhaps you are not able to be a monk; it is not your way. Because you can flow with energy better than you can control energy. Then, monkhood is not necessarily for you. With the lay community, I think that basically, let us say, the opportunity to practice toward enlightenment is equally available for the lay community and for the monastery, the community of monks.

L.M.: You are trying to do that here with the Ligmincha Institute.

T.W.: That is my hope. You know, we don't have a monastery here. And I don't want a monastery here either. Our center is here to provide, for people who are living ordinary lives; it is here to provide them with a place to practice; and to learn, to practice—and to try to integrate that practice into their lives as much as they are able to.

L.M.: Is the goal of liberation possible for the lay practitioner even in this very lifetime? That seems to be a hallmark of Bon Dzogchen teachings.

T.W.: Dzogchen teachings generally say about it happening in one lifetime—that it is "one body, one life"—it means you can achieve full liberation.

L.M.: You can, yes, but it still depends. You have to take the practice very seriously.

T.W.: You have to take the practice very seriously. But not intensely; rather, you do it with joy, and without tension. When people talk about being serious, they lose the joy.

L.M.: So how do you have joy?

T.W.: You have to have a joyful attitude toward practice.

L.M.: How do you encourage them as a teacher? Say you might see a student taking a too intense approach.

T.W.: Yes, you try as a teacher, you try to support them; you try to look at the conditions and circumstances of the student. And you try to guide them as much as possible. Some students might have a past karmic connection, and they immediately connect with the teachings. They immediately feel at home there; they practice, they become very successful. But some students, they are very hard to work with. But still, with them it might be possible. And then, other people don't have a karmic connection at all. So there is nothing you can do, except that you can make a new karmic connection. So that in the future, in another lifetime, it is possible.

L.M.: Their own history, their past karmas perhaps are an obstacle for them to do the practice.

T.W.: Sure, we all go—we have all been in school. There we take different subjects, have different majors because of interests, similar karmic connections and abilities; it opens up different doors for different people. It is the same thing with the *dharma*, the teachings, also.

L.M.: Can someone, through the practice and through unselfish action, can they shed that karmic weight you might call it, that we have been conditioned with? A student comes with not such good karma, but still the teacher sees their sincerity.

T.W.: They can be, they can be; the teacher can help and guide them. They can try to work through purification practices; and they can overcome their deficiencies. Still, there are people, it is very hard to work with them; they don't have a connection.

L.M.: What is your role as a teacher of Bon? Also, how does a potential student know that the teacher really is who they say they are—and that the teacher is right for them?

T.W.: Well, I think one way is—the role of the the teacher, the compassion of the teacher. It somehow pervades and enters into the student's consciousness—when you meet—and even before you meet. The student starts to have dreams, for example—it is not a coincidence—people start to have dreams about you. You are already connected energy-wise. The students are awakening inside themselves. And when you encounter these students, it is like recognizing an old friend. Immediately, they feel a connection.

L.M.: The teacher feels this.

T.W.: Both teacher and student.

L.M.: Both.

T.W.: When you feel like that, it is a much easier process. There are clear structures in our tradition, as far as the practice is concerned. What is the first thing that you do? You do a preliminary practice. A preliminary practice means that you should take refuge; students should take refuge. That means,

I am committed to your teaching: I follow you; you are my guide. The forms of refuge in which you take refuge are the Buddha, the Dharma, the Sangha. And when you take refuge, you make a more formal connection; once you make a formal connection, then the teacher will try to explain things like impermanence. What does impermanence mean? Life is not the way you think; it is constant change. The only thing that is permanent is change.

L.M.: That's right.

T.W.: If you expect that things should always be the way they are now, then you are deluded. So it is not only explaining the teachings. But showing and looking around, looking at your life: what you hear; what you read in the newspaper; what you see on television—what you see around yourself. How many people that you used to know, how many are left now? How many people every day you hear about—and your close ones too—are dying. It is explaining change and impermanence, and that somehow you are not completely deluding yourself with this world.

You are trying more to understand things from the point of view of the higher Dzogchen teaching. As students understand more and more of these teachings, they are making more of a foundation for themselves. That here I am a guest, I am a traveling guest who is stopping here.

The primary focus becomes more on their practice; the primary focus becomes more on their path—helping other people, helping oneself. So that slowly, slowly, there is development. We call it ripening oneself. As people ripen themselves—through these practices of refuge; *bodichitta*; compassion; impermanence; and offerings and rituals—they will try to go to the higher level. There is the introduction to the nature of mind; and then they go to the higher level, to the visionary practices. Gradually, they become to some extent illuminated.

L.M.: How important is the student's own effort? You could think: Oh, my teacher is so great, so famous. I don't have to do anything, I'm saved.

T.W.: The student should realize that the main thing is that the work is between both teacher and student; not only the teacher. Sometimes people go into a temple, or church, and they simply say: save me. That idea is not very helpful. In a sense, you can ask in that way. But that doesn't mean that you don't take responsibility too.

L.M.: With the Ligmincha community, you are expanding the center and its outreach. Is the community of Bon practitioners which you call the *sangha*, is it essential?

T.W.: Yes, community is essential in the teachings. The essence of the community is the dharma, the teaching. That is a uniting place. Different individuals come together because they follow the same teaching. The teacher too is representing the teaching. Both teacher and student follow together the same teaching; the same message where everybody feels connected. Their hearts feel connected to the teaching. That brings people together, in order that every individual has that experience of closeness to the teaching. And that needs support. If you live in places, in big cities where you don't have any sangha support, it is very hard to survive. For instance, you have a friend who likes to golf; you like to golf; and your sport is supported by your friends. But you don't have support for your practice.

L.M.: To meditate.

T.W.: Yes, to meditate. If you don't have support, then your meditation doesn't grow and develop. Sangha is very, very important.

L.M.: We do make mistakes as we practice; probably almost everyone makes their fair share of mistakes along the way. How does the teacher help the student get back on track?

T.W.: When the connection between the teacher and student is very close, that guidance can take place easily. When they are not very connected, then the guidance is not effective.

L.M.: As the teacher, do you see students making mistakes, even when they may be shy about telling you?

T.W.: Sure, sure, you can always see the student and understand how their practice is going. If you are close enough, you can definitely help. Sometimes people ask, they write.

L.M.: You get quite a lot of correspondence?

T.W.: A lot.

L.M.: According to Bon Dzogchen teachings, and in your own experience, just what constitutes the good life—and the good death?

T.W.: What is the good life: it is to be able to live fully. That means being—not to be controlled by one's own dualistic confusion. You are able to live more fully. That is not to say in a bigger house, or a smaller house. Or, what kind of dress I wear, or how much I have in the bank. It's not that. To live fully, without conditioning oneself—within one's own mind; and amid circumstances around oneself. You can be affected sometimes by others. You go out and somebody says to you: you're wearing a green jacket; that doesn't look good. What does that do to you? For the next two hours, you are depressed. Constantly, you can be affected by the circumstances around you. That is not a good life.

You need to have some stability in yourself. And that stability within yourself has very much to do with the recognition of the nature of mind—the recognition of oneself, the recognition of one's own base. What is my base, who am I? Once I recognize that, then I am not too dependent on other people's opinion. Instead you understand what you feel; you can help them in what they are feeling. But you are not dependent on that. I think the good life is like that. And on the basis of that, when you live like that, you are able to help other people. Because you are able to see more clearly. You are not caught up in your own ideas, in your thoughts and emotions. You are more for other people, you are more able to help them through your compassion and love. I consider that is living well.

L.M.: Yes, I often think that society encourages us to see each other as consumers, as objects. If I do this for you today, what will you do for me next week?

T.W.: Exactly—just do something that needs to be done. Somebody needs to do it. If it is the case that it is for you to do, just do it. Don't expect anything back. Of course it's not easy for us not to expect anything back—but minimizing that.

L.M.: You use the phrase: the nature of mind. Is mind then to be considered something different from what it is commonly thought to be in Western psychology? There it often seems that the mind is connected literally, physically to the brain; it's a materialistic, mechanistic approach. Bon says the mind is a much more embracing reality.

T.W.: Mind is much more full. We don't think about the brain. We think about the heart. Some of our thoughts may come from the brain, perhaps. But mind—and the nature of mind—is also different. Mind is, you know, constantly moving. The nature of mind is at the base of those movements.

L.M.: But the practice will get one to see beyond all the moving?

T.W.: If you are connected to yourself, you will be less driven by your thoughts; but, if you are not connected to yourself, you will be easily driven by your thoughts. Your thoughts are part of your mind.

L.M.: You also employ a mantra?

T.W.: Yes.

L.M.: Is that a preliminary practice, a part of concentration?

T.W.: Yes.

L.M.: Is that similar to yogic concentration, the constant repetition of a mantra—and is it done audibly?

T.W.: Either way.

L.M.: Depending on what the student needs to do.

T.W.: It depends on what you are reciting in your mantra. Usually your mantras are more sounded aloud, most of them. But there are some cases where they are activated by vibrations inside.

L.M.: Inside—and then, what about the good death?

T.W.: Death is—the good death is—where, when you are dying, it is being able to die free. Again, it is the same way: able to live free, able to die free.

That means, what is happening is—it is death. And completely, how do you say, you . . .

L.M.: Embrace.

T.W.: Embrace *the* death.

L.M.: You embrace death, you don't try to push it away.

T.W.: You don't push—because the meaning of it fully is, you have embraced the death. It is not something else; it doesn't mean that it is bad. But if you have a problem with death, it means you have a problem. In the West, what sometimes with these new-age things, people are trying to say is: Oh, death is not death. They make different meanings out of things. That is always, always feeding the fear of the dualistic mind; rather, than making them recognize what it really is, the truth. And then, healing in that way. But these people try to say: Oh, you're not dying.
You are dying. Understand that you are dying. And that dying is not necessarily bad. If you understand that death is fine, natural, then you can heal your death. If you say death is not death—death is another way of life—you are deluding yourself again. In the West, sometimes they feed the fear of death a lot. By putting things at different levels, the way people sell products. They sell at one level; and when it doesn't work, they put a new name on the same product. Still, they are selling the same thing.

L.M.: Is death looked at differently in the East?

T.W.: I mean that, death is death. So, the good death—a part of the good death—will be a good preparation for death. So you know what the process of death is. What each moment is happening to you when you are dying. And what each thing is, that will happen to you after you die. All these things: what it means to you; how you relate to them—how you apply your practice in relation to those intermediate states and visions. That is a good death. A good death is like preparing for the final examination. And then, when you take the examination, it is a good examination because you have prepared well.

L.M.: So while you are living, and not just at the moment of dying, you are doing *bardo* practices?

65

T.W.: Yes, while you are living, you are preparing the practice of death. *Bardo practice, phowa practice, dream practice*—all are in some sense a preparation for death.

L.M.: So that you will be able to let go, joyfully. You will feel joy, rather than fear or pain. Even if someone had a physical illness like cancer that was killing them, they could still through their practice, their attitude, be joyful.

T.W.: Sure, sometimes the pain you have is less than what you think of your pain. Sometimes people have a bad relation to their pain; their relation to the pain kills them, not the pain itself. Pain is just physical pain, it's natural. You are dying, it is death. But you are not struggling with death. It is a more peaceful pain then.

L.M.: In Bon, as in Buddhism, there is no deity, or spiritual guide, or guru, that meets you at death.

T.W.: Well, of course, when you are dying, there is always a support; there is always external support. Moreover, there is the teacher. We call it a near-death introduction. Somebody says: O.K., you know, you're dying, and I am here to help you. You remember what you need to do for the process of death. Your elements are dissolving; you are losing your physical abilities; you are losing your body ability. Now you are dissipating your body heat. Your blood energy is disappearing; your breath is disappearing. Everything is dissolving.

L.M.: Can the teacher accompany the student in their death even if they are geographically apart?

T.W.: If somebody is somewhere else, we pray. We pray as a group. I pray for my students. I do a phowa practice that is able to transfer their consciousness to a higher level. That is what we do. If I am close enough, I try to help them by visiting in person.

L.M.: Part of this understanding death correctly is that consciousness in fact is not obliterated. The individual who dies just goes to a different level of existence.

T.W.: Yes, they will be reborn somewhere else. It is not like they are disappearing completely; they will be reborn.

L.M.: Although they think they will no longer exist, and that accounts for much of their fear?

T.W.: No, not as a Tibetan. They don't think that way; Westerners, they might. We Tibetans think, we pray for a better rebirth. It is a little different. If you die as a human, you can be born back as a human. Or you can be born in a hell. Or, you can be born in a heaven. It always depends on what you have done in your past. It shows, it determines, your future.

L.M.: Could you be reborn as an animal, or in a nonhuman form?

T.W.: Yes, you can be born as an animal too.

L.M.: But for someone who joyfully does the practice, and who tries to lead a good life, their going down into an animal birth usually wouldn't be necessary?

T.W.: Yes, that's right.

L.M.: Today we are living in a very fluid environment, and there is a lot of interaction among the religions. Just forty years ago, you might have thought there was only Protestant, Catholic, and Jew in America. Now we have had since the sixties a wide array of Eastern teachings being made available. What kind of opportunities do you see now for dialogue among the world religions—East and West?

T.W.: I think sometimes that for different religious leaders it might not be so easy to have interreligious dialogue, because of certain beliefs and differences. Still, I think that for many people who do enter into this dialogue, that it is a healing experience. And that the initial discomfort disappears. Having tolerance for differences—for unity and diversity as they call it—seems to be important. You believe in that, I believe in this; yet we respect each other. I am not afraid of you, you are not afraid of me. There might be some things you do, they might be really good to do. So I learn from that. People can have exchanges, that is a very natural thing. And all those changes will benefit human beings.

L.M.: I know that you have met with other teachers.

T.W.: I have been working with some Jewish people down in Houston; also with Native Americans.

L.M.: Are they living out West?

T.W.: Yes, in the West, with Hopis, Sioux, and other tribes. And I was down in Mexico visiting shamans just a month ago.

L.M.: Do you find that you have, that Bon has, quite a few parallels, commonalities with them?

T.W.: A lot, a lot.

L.M.: It's not that you're thinking that they ought to convert to Bon religion. You go there to learn and interact.

T.W.: In some cases, you learn from other persons; in other cases, the other person learns from you.

L.M.: If one is Christian or Jewish, for instance, might that person benefit from the Bon teaching, yet still continue in their religion?

T.W.: It depends on how much they want to commit themselves. There are different levels of commitment. One level of commitment is full; it is not that I am committed here a little bit, and there a little bit. No, I am with my whole body, mind, and speech, and my soul, committed to this tradition. In Buddhism, you take refuge; in Bon, you take refuge. You are committed compeletely, a hundred percent. That level of commitment means that you really become a part of it; then you are not a part of anything else.

L.M.: Yes.

T.W.: That doesn't mean you exclude anything. You pay respect to everything, but practice-wise, it's just that one practice. It is good in any tradition if people feel that way; I think that is the best. But there are a lot of people who don't know what they themselves are—they only know what their parents are.

L.M.: That's an important point.

T.W.: I think it doesn't mean that: Oh, my family is Jewish, so I should be Jewish. I want to study Buddhism just to study it; but I want to remain Jewish because my parents are that. That is not a good enough reason. Because who we are originally, our parents don't make that decision. If you trace back, you probably were a nun at one time. I think it is really important to understand what you feel at this time in your life. You feel like you just want to do a little bit of this, a little bit of that. Now somebody can advise you that maybe it would be good to focus on one thing. But you don't feel that way.

It is all right of course. The Ligmincha center, our center, is welcoming to people like that. Anybody who wants to learn is welcome; anybody who wants to practice is welcome. But as you move through the tradition, you get to a certain point with the teachings when it is important to commit yourself.

L.M.: Do most people who come here make a commitment?

T.W.: They don't.

L.M.: Most don't fully commit themselves.

T.W.: No, but there are people who do; there are people who don't. I'm talking a lot about what is happening. I am also talking about what should happen.

L.M.: So let's say someone decides to make a full commitment to Bon. Could they continue being Catholic or being Jewish?

T.W.: If you are fully committed to being a Catholic, then you should be Catholic, not Jewish.

L.M.: I mean Bon.

T.W.: I'm saying it doesn't matter, it's the same thing. It doesn't relate only with Buddhism or Bon. I mean a Catholic can always learn from Jewish religion, a Jew can learn from a Catholic. Bon can learn from Buddhists. An interchange of learning and education is always fine. As far as following something very seriously goes, I think it is very important to follow one path. It is not a question of one is better, and one is less good. It is just because of the commitment level—and time. It is like a family. If you have a relationship, you cannot say that I am being with you now, but also, I am across town. With another family; you cannot have two kinds of relationships like that. A relationship between a man and woman is similar.

L.M.: It is like a spiritual marriage.

T.W.: Yes, in some sense it is a spiritual marriage.

L.M.: Do some people who come initially and only want to make a partial commitment—do they gradually come to make a full commitment?

T.W.: Or, they leave.

L.M.: Or they go. Well that is . . .

T.W.: Nature.

L.M.: One of those things.

T.W.: Divorce rate is very high in this country.

L.M.: A teacher will still have good wishes for the student who leaves.

T.W.: Sure, of course.

L.M.: You aren't personally disappointed; you are detached, knowing that the person is still ruled by their mind.

T.W.: It depends on what kind of relation the teacher has with that person. There are so many hundreds that come and go. If you feel bad about it with everybody, you will be sick and dead. But sometimes, if you have certain expectations from a student; and you feel that the student has understood something of what you are trying to communicate; and then, you find out it was not true, that is disappointing.

L.M.: Westerners often take an approach with Eastern teachers that puts the teacher on a pedestal. Teachers are treated like God, really, they aren't supposed to feel any emotions.

T.W.: A fantasy—the teacher should never be sick.

L.M.: How does the Bon meditation practice of the *Six Lokas* help us deal with negative emotions? One of the things that makes life so complicated here in the West is that our emotions are afflicted; we often seem at cross purposes with ourselves.

T.W.: Basically, what the meditation of the Six Lokas does is—that you just try to burn the seeds of different afflicted emotions—try to understand these negative emotions as afflictions that cause suffering—before they actually take form. So there might be people who are suffering, who are living in a bad neighborhood—suffering due to the outcome, or result, of anger in their life. They have so much anger; they make bad decisions; they are poor. They get into a bad neighborhood where things are broken and there is a lot of anger around. So before you are being born there, you can in some sense burn the seed of anger within yourself. Then you will live in peaceful places, rather than in rough places.

We believe there are six different dimensions or realms of different beings. For example, you are born here as a human being, you have causes and conditions to be born here. For fifty, sixty years you are living here. What you are doing is, you are burning your human karma. The only problem is that, while you are burning your karma, exhausting your karma in order to be free from that karma, you also are reaccumulating karma.

L.M.: Making new karma.

T.W.: Making new ones, preparing for the next life. If you are not accumulating new ones, then you will be free when you are dead.

L.M.: You will be free.

T.W.: In a lot of things you will be free.

L.M.: Bon practice is to help the student learn how not to create new karmic webs or entanglements.

T.W.: Not to create new karmic waves. And to try to burn the seeds of the old ones.

L.M.: Which must be very substantial.

T.W.: Many lives.

L.M.: Over the course of many lifetimes. Then too, Bon meditation stands on its own as a tradition. Though it has been obviously influenced by Buddhism over many centuries.

T.W.: Bon is a form of Buddhism. But it has its unique characteristics.

L.M.: Perhaps what it all comes down to—by our daily practice—is that we are really learning to love more. Of course, that's the teaching of Jesus, to love one another.

T.W.: Yes, I think the main thing is really being an example oneself for other people. If you don't like suffering, you know other people don't like suffering. If you don't like pain, if you don't want to be hurt: don't hurt other people. If you don't want bad things said to you—don't say them to other people.

Whatever you want, other people want that. So a learning place would be—a good place to begin would be—with the example of oneself, how you feel.

CONTEMPLATIVE PRAYER WITH EDWARD McCORKELL

L.M.: How would you describe contemplative, or Centering, prayer in the Christian meditation tradition?

E.M.: The Christian or Catholic tradition of contemplative prayer is taught by some of the great church fathers and theologians. But the tradition of contemplative prayer goes even further back to the beginnings of Christianity. It begins with Pentecost, as we read in the Acts of the Apostles. The Holy Spirit came down upon the apostles, this rather motley crew, the first disciples of Jesus. They were united in this wonderful spirit, and that was the launching of the Christian church.

The key had been made clear by Jesus himself when he said: "The Holy Spirit will teach you all things." The Gospel of John, in particular, provides us with a very good context for understanding the nature of Christian meditation.

L.M.: The Gospel of John.

E.M.: Especially, in the Last Supper talk—we're talking about chapters 14, 15, and 16 of John, where Jesus gives us the final discourse of the Last Supper.

There we have the nucleus, the heart of the Christian tradition of mystical, contemplative prayer. Jesus speaks there of being led from discipleship to friendship, and into a more intimate relationship. The person of the Trinity who our Lord emphasized as crucial and central was the Holy Spirit. In any presentation of Christian prayer, the Holy Spirit is essential. There have been over the centuries various methods of meditation. For instance, Saint Ignatius of Loyola, the founder of the Jesuits, introduced a form of meditation that is like the threshold of contemplative prayer.

L.M.: That would be more reflection, spiritual reflection.

E.M.: Reflection, meditation—it follows reading. One goes from the reading of sacred texts to meditation.

L.M.: *Lectio divina.*

E.M.: Yes, *lectio*—and meditation, pondering on the word of scripture. This is an active type of contemplation in our Christian tradition; most types of Catholic prayer can be classified as active contemplation. Passive contemplation is really, strictly speaking, contemplative, or Centering, prayer.

In contemplative prayer, we are not praying so much to God, as we do in the liturgy. The four parts or elements of the liturgy that we find in the Mass are petition, adoration, reparation, and thanksgiving. They are easy to remember as "part."

L.M.: Right, "part."

E.M.: With the celebration of the Eucharist, that is still active contemplation; one uses words, gestures, and so forth. Contemplative prayer is, in contrast, wordless and nonconceptual. That is hard for a Westerner to deal with; we're so conceptual and analytical in our Western culture. The average Westerner has to divest himself or herself of the habitual attitude of analyzing everything and trying to figure it out intellectually.

We do need to have a basic doctrinal and biblical foundation in which we build our life of prayer—this intimate relationship with God. However, this relationship is something that transcends our normal, human faculties—it is supernatural. It has a foundation in our two faculties of mind and will; they will have to come into play.

L.M.: We bring them in.

E.M.: They're essential. But as one's relationship with God develops, and evolves, and becomes more intimate, we become less and less analytical. The love faculty—which is mainly in the will—will take over, and will predominate. In its perfection, growth, and development, contemplative, or Centering, prayer in the Christian tradition is essentially in the will. Though it is based on faith and the intellect, and includes the reading of sacred scripture.

L.M.: We don't want to abandon all that, and just meditate.

E.M.: Yet one goes beyond that, as one becomes more familiar with Christ. One then moves into the affective dimension—of surrendering oneself to Christ; one enters into a relationship of love.

L.M.: You meditate every day, and you practice contemplative or Centering Prayer.

E.M.: Yes, for many years as novice director, I taught the method of Centering Prayer to novices here at Holy Cross Abbey. I instructed them to do Centering Prayer for a minimum of one hour every day, and to do it in two half-hour periods. There is one period in the morning, which the whole monastic community does. For the novices, I added another half-hour period before vespers. So that during their novitiate formation, the first two years of their monastic life, they would develop the habit of doing Centering Prayer for a minimum of one hour.

L.M.: Do they do it in the small meditation chapel?

E.M.: It could be done either in the small meditation chapel, or in their own cell, which might be quieter.

75

L.M.: It's good to meditate alone, too.

E.M.: That's what I insisted on.

L.M.: How long have you been doing contemplative prayer?

E.M.: For many, many years; even before I became novice master I was doing this.

L.M.: Back when you were abbot here?

E.M.: Twenty or thirty years ago.

L.M.: And when you were serving as abbot at the monastery in Chile, back in the sixties?

E.M.: Yes. When I entered the monastery over fifty years ago, there was a half-hour of silent prayer in the morning, and fifteen minutes in the afternoon with vespers. My own experience is that fifteen minutes is not long enough. Though one hour is too long for many Westerners in one session.

L.M.: For Hindus and Buddhists it's no problem.

E.M.: They're geared to that by their own temperament. So two half-hour periods of contemplative prayer is what I recommend. More recently, I have been teaching Centering Prayer to a lot of retreatants at our guest house.

L.M.: Lay people.

E.M.: Yes, lay people. A good example or symbol of this prayer is dance. I was attending the ballet, and there was this ballerina; she couldn't have been more than 18 or 19 years old—she danced beautifully. And as I observed and watched her movement, I received this inspiration. My own personal concept of the divine life of the Trinity, and the image I find most satisfying to describe it is that of the Father, Son, and Holy Spirit dancing in a circle—an infinite circle of love. God is infinite, and all the universe, the earth we're on, and all the other planets and stars, are in this great cosmic dance. And beyond this finite, created universe, there is this infinite circle of God. In contemplative prayer, we're not praying to God, we're not thinking what we should say. We are partners with God in this dance, this circle.

L.M.: There's no external activity on our part.

E.M.: That's right. We are dynamically active, spiritually speaking; but we're not dancing physically.

L.M.: But the breath is part of this.

E.M.: The breath is a physical reality, and it is a symbol of what is taking place. The spirit is invisible, intangible; yet Jesus became flesh. We can understand him because he has become incarnate; we can understand the Father because Jesus gave us the most beautiful portrait of him in the story of the prodigal son.

L.M: A portrait of his compassion.

E.M.: He is compassionate toward the son, he ran to meet him.

L.M.: Some see the person of the Holy Spirit as feminine, as the feminine aspect of the trinity.

E.M.: Yes, it is for me, definitely. The feminine dimension of God is revealed in the Holy Spirit and not in the Father and the Son.

L.M.: Why is that so?

E.M.: Neither the Father or the Son is a feminine figure. The Holy Spirit has a nurturing mission—it nurtures that spiritual life in us, and reveals itself to us. Now I don't say herself. I would like to say herself, but I would probably be reported to the local bishop, or to Rome if I did.

L.M.: The word is out now.

E.M.: So that's it then. Now regarding this prayer, if you can just sit in your chair and enter into this half-hour, into the silence of contemplative prayer.

L.M.: Does one just sit upright and keep the posture straight?

E.M.: I advise people that as far as posture is concerned to use the prayer bench. Young people may not need a stool. But for others, I say just put that prayer bench under you. The thing is to have a straight back. For contemplative prayer, one doesn't want to be in a painful posture.

L.M.: The correct posture is essential.

E.M.: You have to keep the body still. Though, you also have the intellect.

L.M.: The mind.

E.M.: In Western culture especially, the intellect is the problem; we're very analytical. That is where we need to use the prayer word as a help. I like Father or *Abba*, God is Father or *Abba*—or Jesus can be used, love can be used. The word expresses one's relationship with God. It doesn't have to be repeated every minute; except when one's mind is drifting, or when a thought develops.

L.M.: To bring you back to the center. Is that done along with the breath?

E.M.: The breath, of course. You get into the habit of doing that and it is going on all the time.

L.M.: There's no exaggerated effort.

E.M.: No, it is gentle and deep, but slow. It is gentle, but without straining. One must have the right practice of breathing deeply; we're just not thinking of our breathing.

L.M.: It is this movement of love.

E.M.: Exactly. After one has done it for some time and developed the practice, it comes more easily.

L.M.: The mind continues to do its thing.

E.M.: That's right. We don't let that tendency to analyze everything take over where we are thinking: How well am I doing?

L.M.: Or, what am I going to do later on?

E.M.: Something like that. The prayer word is a great help to recenter ourselves, and it also helps us get interiorly cleared out of a lot of distractions and images. Though it is impossible to be totally blank.

L.M.: That doesn't happen.

E.M.: If one is aware that we are in a dynamic movement within the Trinity, that in itself serves to put away other thoughts. Be consciously aware of the fact that we are caught up in this circle of the Trinity. That you are in this dance with God.

L.M.: We are partners with God.

E.M.: Partners, exactly; so we want to surrender.

L.M.: We don't actually see Jesus, or the Holy Spirit, when we meditate.

E.M.: No, no, you don't try to image them.

L.M.: We are in darkness, this personal darkness.

E.M.: Yes, you are in darkness. Usually, you close your eyes. That shuts out all external images, though the imagination gets into the act. Images will come onto our mental screen and then we just have to deal with them. The way to overcome these things is not to attack them.

L.M.: We build them up even more that way.

E.M.: Contemplative prayer is like the pole on a carousel that is stable, still, and firm. On a merry-go-round, it is the only still point; the rest is going round and round and round. That is the way our life is: going, going, and more going. But now we're coming to the center. Because of our fallen human nature, we drift off, we drift off from the center.

L.M.: The present moment. Now is it important to have a teacher for learning contemplative prayer?

E.M.: It is a help to have a teacher.

L.M.: Here at the monastery the lay people learn this form of meditative prayer from you.

E.M.: I teach it all the time at the retreat house. I have all these married people for the most part learning contemplative prayer. I also give them a short reading list of Keating, Merton, and others. And then, they get right into doing the practice.

L.M.: Do they check in with you periodically about their practice?

E.M.: They come twice a year for retreats. People I counsel at the guest house also end up learning Centering Prayer. You often first have to address their life problems and help them out. But then inevitably, no matter what the problem or the need is, I end up introducing them to Centering Prayer.

L.M.: Do you think contemplative or Centering Prayer is being taught at other Trappist monasteries?

E.M.: I don't know specifically, but I'm sure a good deal of it is going on.

L.M.: How about the teaching of Centering Prayer in local parishes— would that be a good idea?

E.M.: If I were a parish priest, I would teach the people from the pulpit, and also make available literature on Centering Prayer.

L.M.: There could be a place in the parish for Centering Prayer groups that meet on a regular basis.

E.M.: Yes, sure. One of the great fruits of the Second Vatican Council is the "universal call to holiness." Everyone is called to holiness: married people, mothers and fathers, single people. People living in the secular world are called, not just monks.

Though monks and nuns in contemplative orders give a special emphasis to this.

L.M.: Like the Trappists here. Do you think that Jesus himself practiced contemplative prayer when he went up to the mountain to experience some necessary solitude?

E.M.: Exactly, I'm glad you bring that up, that is very important. Jesus did get tired; he was human. He had to get away from the crowd. Now if he had to do that, how much more we should need to do so. Many people say that: Well, he was just doing it to set an example. But he had to do it. He was not just setting an example; though he was also doing that. He was making very clear that the human condition is such that we all require solitude, and quiet, and silence. And in order that we might enter into this intimate relationship with God through contemplative prayer.

L.M.: You said that you still do yoga exercises every day.

E.M.: I do yoga every morning because I am convinced of the importance of the body—that it be conditioned as an instrument of the spirit, rather than an obstacle. Diet is important, the right kind of food and not to be over-weight. Also, breathing and posture, especially deep breathing. We have tremendous capacity to breathe and yoga helps with that.

L.M.: Often we don't breathe deeply.

E.M.: Normally, we don't. But in yoga we learn breathing exercises. Then one is more awake and alert. When people doze off, it's because they're not breathing deeply, it's superficial breathing. In fact, the process of breathing is a very good symbol for the movement of the spirit in contemplative prayer.

L.M.: We are centering on the spirit.

E.M.: We are doing it in the communion of saints; we are not alone in all this.

L.M.: They are with us.

81

E.M.: In this dance with all the saints.

L.M.: It reminds me of the "sacred conversation" in a Fra Angelico painting.

E.M.: We just allow ourselves to be, and join the dance that has been going on for all time.

L.M.: Merton talked about taking part in the general dance, the dance of the spirit.

E.M.: We join the dance. But it's not a jitterbug you know; it's more like a waltz, or ballet. There is nothing violent or laborious about contemplative prayer. Some people are not attracted to this, and they say that it's too much work. No, the whole point is that it is very relaxing. Yet, because we are so westernized—and think you can't get anything without labor—people really try to make it work. That way of thinking is a real obstacle to contemplative prayer. One has to learn to relax.

L.M.: You do yoga headstands too.

E.M.: Yes, every day, that is important for the circulation of the blood. Even just breathing exercises are a great help in doing contemplative prayer. I would recommend that we integrate the spiritual with the physical.

L.M.: We really need to do that. I also think it's important that you are presenting this in a Christian context. We often think of this concern with the body and breath as only being Hindu, or Eastern. Though the desert fathers, and probably the hesychast tradition in the Orthodox church, apparently used yogic postures and breathing techniques; and, of course, a mantralike word.

E.M.: Now, when one sits in this silent prayer a thought will come, or an image may come, through a noise we hear. Many mornings here at the monastery we hear a train; it is a nice sound, the whistle of a train. I like the sound of the train, and it doesn't become a distraction to me. It reminds me of the journey I'm on.

L.M.: Many people in the city will hear a lot more noises.

E.M.: That is why I advise people to do contemplative prayer early in the morning.

L.M.: After a good night's sleep.

E.M.: Before the day gets underway, and before you go to work, start the day with contemplative prayer. Make your morning prayers short; take five minutes or so saying the morning offering. Don't attempt to say longer prayers like the whole rosary at that time. You want to devote that first half-hour of the day to contemplative prayer. Actually, you know it's bad that most priests don't get any training in this form of prayer while attending seminary.

L.M.: Do you think they should?

E.M.: They should receive that. And in fact, if I were a bishop, which I'll never be, thanks to God, I would insist on a year of spiritual formation. We have two years of novitiate here at the monastery, and all religious orders provide at least a year. Seminaries aren't doing that. They have two years of philosophy, and four years of theology. They should also have an intensive year spent in spiritual formation. I understand that some bishops are considering this.

L.M.: The bishops, too, ought to be doing contemplative prayer.

E.M.: The laity are the ones who are taking the lead in all this. They seem to be more receptive; they are better disciples. Seminarians are trained to be teachers and preachers, but not disciples.

L.M.: We are all called to be disciples.

E.M.: You could call it an occupational hazard. A teacher is always talking to others and always preaching and teaching.

L.M.: You have been quite involved in the East-West dialogue among Christians and Buddhists, and between Christians and Hindus. How do you

83

think there can be more harmony, understanding, and respect among the world religions and spiritual traditions? I know you have participated in a contemplative congress with the Dalai Lama.

E.M.: I was at one of those in California. I have also been involved in the East-West dialogue for a number of years along with Thomas Keating. It all came about after Vatican II, when a new ponifical council for interreligious dialogue was established in Rome for the first time. They began by asking: Where do we begin this dialogue—with Buddhism, Hinduism, with Moslems?

L.M.: With Judaism.

E.M.: There has been a dialogue with Judaism for many years.

L.M: So then, with non-Western religions.

E.M.: After much discussion, it was noted that what we have in common with Buddhists and Hindus are monks. So they said, we must bring the monks together. That was in 1967—the next year 1968, the first interreligious meeting of monastics was held in Bangkok. Merton was there; he was invited as an outstanding Western monk.

L.M.: He wrote a lot about, and actively encouraged this dialogue.

E.M.: Merton went and spent quite a bit of time with the Dalai Lama in India before going on to Bangkok. He has written in his book *The Asian Journal* about the final mystical experience he had in that grotto—which has three great stone buddhas, in Sri Lanka.

L.M.: Polonnaruwa.

E.M.: Yes, Polonnaruwa. There was this diocesan priest waiting nearby, who had driven Merton to this famous site, and he must have thought: What is that man doing over there with those idols? Well, Merton was actually having a mystical experience. He came to realize that ultimately, the streams of the different religions of Buddhism, Hinduism, and Christianity would converge one day.

84

L.M.: One of the figures there is Ananda, a chief disciple of the Buddha.

E.M.: Merton experienced at that moment a special grace. He recognized that the same Holy Spirit of truth and love is guiding and directing the Buddhist, and the Hindu, and the Muslim—as we Christians are, through Jesus. We don't have a monopoly on the Holy Spirit. The common denominator in the world religions is the Holy Spirit.

L.M.: It's not just Catholic, it is universal.

E.M.: No, it's not just Catholic or Christian.

L.M.: Is it important to cultivate personal friendships with people of other religions?

E.M.: Yes, there is a meeting of hearts. There may not quite be a meeting of minds—since there are different philosophies and ways of expressing them.

L.M.: The religions have their own very different theological underpinnings.

E.M.: But there is a meeting on a deeper level.

L.M.: Do you find this dialogue between East and West encourages more understanding, and less of a "I'm right, you don't have the truth" approach?

E.M.: That's right. As time goes by and we meet together, we pray together for half an hour in silent prayer.

L.M.: Christians together with Buddhists, Hindus.

E.M.: You become conscious, you become very much aware, that we're all in this together. That the same Holy Spirit of truth and love is in my Hindu brother, and in my Buddhist brother with me. The Holy Spirit is not confined to the Christian way. We feel that it is the way for us, since God has become incarnate in Jesus Christ. At the same time, God is incarnate in these other religions. And in some of their leaders, such as Buddha.

L.M.: There are other great traditions of saints and gurus, such as the Sikh religion and the bhakti saints of India. And for instance the bodhisattvas in Mahayana Buddhism.

E.M.: Exactly, there is a kind of communion of saints in their tradition as well.

L.M.: Not that the Holy Spirit plans for them all to become Catholic or Christian at some future time.

E.M.: No, not at all, that's the whole thing we have to get away from—the idea that we've got to convert everybody to Christianity. That is not the direction to go. And personally, I don't think that Jesus expects that.

L.M.: Right, I don't think that is what Jesus' ministry is all about.

E.M.: He wants us to make him known to those who want to know more about Christ, and to share the New Testament teaching of Jesus with them. The most powerful means of evangelization is example; it's not preaching. There is a famous Latin text that says: "*Verba sonat, exempla tonat.*" Words sound, but example thunders. People will remark after the Mass, "beautiful sermon, they preached lovely." But then if you ask them what did the priest say, they can't even remember.

L.M.: That is funny.

E.M.: One of the persons who had the greatest impact upon me was when I was a young boy of seven and first started serving Mass.

L.M.: Back in your native South Africa.

E.M.: This woman was there every morning at Mass, Miss Newman was her name, a fairly old lady. She was always there, and she was praying all the time. When everybody was coming in for Mass, she was in her prayer; and when Mass was over, she was still in prayer. She was a contemplative. And she was probably one of the sources of my vocation. When I think about it and talk about it now, I can see that maybe those were the first seeds of my contemplative vocation. I thought as a young man that I was going to be a Paulist missionary and preach the gospel. But God had in mind that I will be a contemplative monk.

And in my own family, my father was a beautiful person and a really holy man. I was fourteen when my father died; and I was serving the Mass on the Sunday after his death. The pastor gave a kind of euology of my father. And I remember him saying that my father was never, ever known to say an unkind word about anyone. Well, I could have got up and told the congregation that I had lived with him, and I knew that was exactly true. That was one thing he would never stand for, if we started criticizing other people and running them down. He would say that in our house, if you don't have a positive word to say, then just shut up.

L.M.: That is beautiful.

E.M.: He wasn't naive, he knew that there was evil in the world and that people weren't always behaving right. But he said we don't talk about that. My father was very gentle, but on that one thing he was very firm. So often people are complaining about one another and criticizing one another: Isn't he awful? Isn't she dreadful? There's so much of that, too much of it.

L.M.: That's part of what creates all the misery and suffering in this world.

E.M.: We would all be better off if the energy that people are using in complaining was spent in contemplative prayer, and with building up a positive attitude of loving kindness, and compassion, and mercy toward others.

L.M.: There is a sense of humor and friendliness that can come out of spiritual practice.

E.M.: Oh, definitely. God help us if we lose our sense of humor. It's often overlooked that Jesus had a real sense of humor.

L.M.: Where do you find him showing it?

E.M.: I'm sure that Jesus laughed regarding Saint Peter. The time that two or three apostles were in the boat fishing, and Jesus came walking on the water. Peter was surprised, but typically, he asked Jesus if he could join him on the water. So Our Lord said: "Come." He invited him, and when Peter stepped out of the boat onto the water—that was an act of faith on his part.

L.M.: Yes, it certainly was.

E.M.: But once he got out on the water, the next step was trust. So he was about to drown because he didn't have trust. It's one thing to make an act of faith in a challenging situation. Then you need more than faith—you've got to have trust. You have got to surrender to Christ; and really believe that the Holy Spirit is going to help you. The second theological virtue is hope. Though that is not very developed in a lot of people. And it's not talked about, and preached about enough.

L.M.: Can we cultivate, and grow, that hope and trust through contemplative prayer?

E.M.: I would think so, that's a good point. All three theological virtues of faith, hope, and love should be exercised and developed in Centering Prayer. Contemplative or Centering Prayer is really an experience—we don't want to use the word activity.

L.M.: We sit there and we're present.

E.M.: The power that comes to us to make an act of faith—and an act of trust—and an act of love—comes from God. Trust is a distinct power. And it's just like muscles. If you don't exercise all the parts of the body, then one particular part gets weak.

L.M.: Does our developing these virtues or powers help us love others more—as Jesus asks us to do?

E.M.: That's what you might call the overflow. The deeper and the more mature our relationship with God becomes, then we are more conditioned to enter into a fruitful relationship with our brothers and sisters.

No matter what their attitude toward us, even if they are negative or prejudiced against us or hostile to us. Then we don't react to them as we normally would due to our fallen, sinful nature.

88

L.M.: That's the hardest thing to do. As Jesus said, resist not evil.

E.M.: He said: "love your enemies, love your enemies." Jesus meant what he said. But we say: love your enemies? Look what he did to me. Look what they've done to me. Well, it doesn't matter what they've done to you. We are really in a sense a kind of lightning rod. It may be nothing personal. But rather, they have some negative self-image, or some past experience from their youth, that we trigger in them. For instance, I may come across as a kind of father-figure. But a person may have a father who is very dominating, and that turns them off to me.

L.M.: You would be an ideal father.

E.M.: I was fortunate to have a beautiful father. My earthly father was a saint, I really believe he was. And my mother too, was a very holy woman. That experience we have of a good father is a tremendous help in relating to our heavenly Father, if one's father has been compassionate and loving. It is very tough for those people whose fathers are tyrants.

L.M.: I understand that you have made friends with people of other religions over the years.

E.M.: Many years ago, I got to know a Hindu friend who was been here for midnight Mass with his family. I met him on a plane when I was coming from Rome, and he was returning from India where his parents were. That was the beginning of a long friendship. He is a very good and devout Hindu, and his wife is Hindu. He shares his Hindu tradition with me, and I have shared the Christian tradition with him. I don't try to make him a Christian.

L.M.: He doesn't try to make you a Hindu either.

E.M.: The first time his wife came here with him was at a Mass in the chapel. When it was time for Holy Eucharist, she got up with everyone else. Though my Hindu friend knew that they shouldn't receive communion. But I was giving out the communion, and when she came up I just gave it to her. I didn't refuse her, though in the past some priests would do that. I knew that this was the right thing to do, and that Jesus wanted me to give himself in the communion host to her.

She wasn't a baptized Christian; but she is God's child. Afterwards of course, her husband informed her that she shouldn't do that. And I explained to her why it is reserved to Catholic and Orthodox Christians. The thing is that they also have a contemplative tradition.

L.M.: The Hindu tradition.

E.M.: My friend's father had given him English translations of some of their sacred books.

L.M.: Such as the Bhagavad Gita.

E.M.: So he passed them on to me and said: This is so you'll know a little more about my religion.

L.M.: Friendship really has a special place in the spiritual journey.

E.M.: This friendship has really been a very great help to me. Even before the Catholic church had entered into this East-West dialogue, I had already got into it with my Hindu friend.

L.M.: Before Vatican II. So perhaps one day you'll get to visit him in India.

E.M.: I would enjoy going to India. I have been thinking how for all these centuries we Cistercians have not had a single monastery in India. Then too, the Trappistine nuns got there first. And now, I'm very happy that Father Francis Acharya, a Belgian monk, and his ashram community at Kurisumala in south India, have recently been admitted into the Cistercian order. That was a dream of mine for many years that we would have houses of both monks and nuns in India.

L.M.: This practice of contemplative prayer, if we're faithful to it, can change our lives.

E.M.: I think that the key to discerning if we are on the right track—that we are truly Christian contemplatives—is that it would be manifested as Jesus said: "By their fruits you will know them." This is especially true in relationships.

Contemplative, or Centering, Prayer is an experience of a deeper relationship with God—as Father, Son, and Holy Spirit. The greatest proof, the acid test you can call it of genuine contemplative prayer, is in our interpersonal relationships. Are they truly charitable, and loving, and compassionate? Compassion is the word that the Hindu and Buddhist traditions use. But even in our Christian tradition, Jesus has said that: "By this all men shall know you are my disciples, that you love one another." One of the most important expressions of love is compassion. That is the entering into the painful experience of another person—and suffering with them. That is compassion.

L.M.: Even with people we don't like, or those who don't like us.

E.M.: One can feel a certain antagonism toward people because they aren't attractive to us. The thing we have to remember is that genuine charity—the charity of the gospel, the charity and love that Jesus taught—is a matter of the will. It is not a matter of emotions or feelings. For me the essential character, or characteristic, of genuine love is the willing the good of the other person. That is essentially what love is. Paul says that the love of God is poured into our hearts by the Holy Spirit. So it is a gift that we ask God to give us—it's not our doing. Genuine love is in the will, and the will can overcome the limitations of feelings.

L.M.: Contemplative prayer can also help us deal with the moments of loneliness we feel in this life.

E.M.: Exactly.

L.M.: That's being out of tune. And we need to be, to get back in tune.

E.M.: That's right. And that is where the trinitarian circle of the Father, Son, and Holy Spirit enables us to overcome that. I don't like to use the word solitude, but solitude is part of that.

L.M.: Solitude can be very positive.

E.M.: But loneliness—we don't have anyone who really loves us, or at least we feel that nobody really loves me. Still, we don't have to worry since we have a far more powerful source of love in God—in particular, in the person of the Holy Spirit. We learn that through the experience of contemplative prayer. The powers of faith, hope, and love are best developed and nurtured through the Eucharist. And we bring to the sacrament of the Eucharist this centeredness, this contemplative awareness. So that we prolong this experience of the Eucharist that only lasts for a few minutes in the morning throughout the day. It is by our being in communion with the Trinity, and then extending beyond our individual experience with God to our brothers and sisters in society.

L.M.: Being in communion with God and with others through contemplative prayer—and through the Eucharist—it is all communion.

E.M.: The Eucharist then becomes the center—not only, of the personal, individual spiritual life which I am living. It is also the source, which enables us to relate to other people we encounter, in our work and in our families.

KRIYA YOGA/ADVAITA VEDANTA WITH SWAMI SHANKARANANDA

S. SHANK: It's a joy to have you here in what I call my blue Himalayas. You see behind you the Blue Ridge mountains of Virginia. We are bringing India to the Blue Ridge; there is a very good view here.

L.M.: Yes, especially along with your serving cups of Indian spice tea. My first question for you is: What are the key meditation teachings and practices you are teaching in the light of Yoga and Advaita Vedanta?

S. SHANK: According to Advaita Vedanta, the nondual philosophy of inclusiveness and nonsectarianism, there are very ancient and very universal mantrams that can easily be traced back to the Vedic times and the Upanishads—as far back as a minimum of 1,500 B.C. Among them are mantrams specifically taught within the Advaita Vedanta tradition that I have been initiated into. They belong to the spiritual heritage, and the guru lineage, that I am part of. There are essentially three mantrams in this tradition that represent gradations, or levels, of experience. The first is called *hamsa*, or *hong swa*. The *hong* is pronounced like *gong*, or *song*; and *swa* is pronounced *shaw*, as in George Bernard Shaw, though it is written as *hamsa*. Hamsa means the swan. Do you know what is special about the swan—and why it is used as a symbol of spirituality?

L.M.: The swan is in the water but not of it, and its feathers stay dry.

S. SHANK: Yes, but it is also credited with being able to separate cream from milk. This is a sign of discrimination. This is intrinsic to the yoga tradition and to spiritual guidance. We must cultivate spiritual discernment, or discrimination, to know the truth. We must be able to separate truth from untruth—or by analogy, the cream, or the essence, from the ocean of milk. Now, we don't know who first revealed this hamsa meditation technique. There are however several references to hamsa in the Svetasvatara Upanishad, which is one of the major ones. And its two references to hamsa clearly indicate that he, Brahma, or the creator, is hamsa. The scripture says that through hamsa meditation, all limitations and delusions are dispelled. Man regains the consciousness of immortality and bliss. It adds that he, Brahma, is dwelling in the city of nine gates—the human body has nine gates, openings, or portals. And Brahma enjoys and perceives the world through these nine gates of the body. That's all it says. The text doesn't explain how the practice was done, and the reason is that when these techniques were given, they were taught only to those who were regarded as qualified—and having been tested. The guru and disciple, or the teacher and student, had to be sure—and the student himself had to be certain—that he was ready.

L.M.: So there was a long apprenticeship.

S. SHANK: Yes, yes.

L.M.: And that was before initiation into hamsa?

S. SHANK: The teacher had to discern this and determine the time when the student was ready. The student would have to repeatedly ask for hamsa initiation to prove his sincerity, perseverance, and commitment. The technique was always given privately and orally—it was never written down. The student was sworn to secrecy—as this is a very sacred and ancient tradition—which still prevails in such ancient orders as the Masonic order.

L.M.: I guess it's a question of having respect for this great treasure of hamsa meditation.

S. SHANK: Thank you, I certainly could not express it better. For thousands of years this hamsa technique has been transmitted as an oral tradition. Now there are those today who take issue with this approach. In American society in particular, there is the belief that anything you want should be instantly available. There should be no obstacle, especially if you are in a position to pay for it. But this is not the spiritual tradition in the Swami Order. It is certainly not a part of the guru line in which I was trained. There a technique is not sold, or given, to someone on demand.

L.M.: Kabir says that if the guru asks for money from the disciple, the disciple should run away as fast as they can from such a guru.

S. SHANK: I salute Kabir for that wisdom and I share wholeheartedly that advice. You cannot put a price on it. But we believe in marketing in this country. That we can market the truth, that we can market meditation techniques. And that the more we charge, obviously the more valuable it must be.

L.M.: It's a premium, a deluxe technique.

S. SHANK: And the quicker it will get you a passport to bliss, and to the kingdom of heaven. That kind of thinking does not promote the sacredness—and the disciplines—that are incumbent on anyone who is serious about self-realization, and on knowing the truth. So to the present day, this hamsa technique is transmitted by word of mouth. That is the first step. Now I can give you the meaning of hamsa without revealing the technique, which is only taught on an individual basis. I have already given you the scriptural reference. Hamsa consists of two words. The first, *hong,* comes from a Sanskrit word *a-hong* which means I, the individual self, the personality, or the finite self.

L.M.: Is that similar to *ahankar?*

S. SHANK: Yes, the ahankar; we have *hong* in that; even though it's written *ahan*, it is ahankar. Now ahankar means the finite self, the egotistic self, or the superimposed self, as it is called in Advaita Vedanta. It is that sensory self which imposes on the nonphysical self—and then proclaims itself to be the identity of who we are—though, mistakenly so.

L.M.: Is that the mind, or the senses?

S. SHANK: It is a complex of mind, senses, and body, or the ahankar.

L.M.: It superimposes this false self.

S. SHANK: It does on consciousness, on the true self.

L.M.: Also, on the atman?

S. SHANK: Yes, on the nonphysical self that I refer to as the nonphysical reality—which is our true identity. The purpose of meditation is to discover one's true identity—whatever meditation technique one uses. Or to rediscover—it is more precise to speak of it as a rediscovery. If it were a discovery, we would be implying that we had never known it before. But rediscovering is, of course, to discover that we have known it before. That what we are seeking is what we discover to be our own self.

L.M.: We have forgotten that.

S. SHANK: We have forgotten that, and it's a forgetfulness that we need to get away from, or come out of. My own research has led me to discern that whoever first was graced by this revelation of hamsa meditation had such an intense yearning to know the truth, and to find out what God really is. Is God then more than what man has been told by others that God is? Can God be experienced directly? That early seeker of truth must have had a passion to explore in depth, and to know more than what had been taught up to that time. Just as if you take two flint stones and rub them together, they will give light, and they will give the spark.

96

L.M.: That was a big family in the cartoon show.

S. SHANK: Oh, the Flintstones? Well, that's where humor comes in, humor and wisdom. So if the flint stones are wet, you cannot get fire out of them. That means as long as one is still waterlogged with sense consciousness, one is not ready to find that inner spark, ignite it, and come in touch with the truth. So this seeker was ready to know the truth. And as he paid attention to his breathing, he became aware that there was an intimate connection between the breath and the mind, or *prana* and thought.

L.M.: So hamsa involves prana?

S. SHANK: Very much so—he came upon the realization that as he observed his inhalation, it disappeared. He discovered that it disappeared into the spiritual center between the eyes.

L.M.: You mean that the prana itself disappears?

S. SHANK: The prana, yes; the sound of the prana.

L.M.: Into the third eye, or spiritual eye?

S. SHANK: Yes, that is located just between and above the eyebrows, nonphysically speaking. He paid attention to it, and naturally wondered what happened.
When prana disappears, where does it go? Well, in that moment even the question disappeared; there was neither question nor answer, but only the moment of awareness.
He was in what we call that point of balance—which is our connection to the inner world, or dimension, or to the unknown.

L.M.: Did it mean that he necessarily saw or heard anything at this point?

S. SHANK: He perceived nothing at that moment. That is what we would call silence—when there is neither thought, nor breath. He experienced that as the exhalation began, the exhalation was no longer hong; it changed to swa. So he pondered: What is the meaning of hamsa? And what is that state that exists between the inhalation and exhalation of the breath? It took him a long time to come to that discernment and realization. It was beyond anything that the mind could contrive, or conjecture, or fabricate. That is why it was a revelation when he got the answer. It happened when the mind was not interfering or creating static.

L.M.: Which the mind normally does all the time.

S. SHANK: That is how we can differentiate between what truly comes from beyond the mind, and what is wishful thinking or manipulation of the mind, or intellect. He discovered, as he continued meditating on hamsa, that hong means I: that I am the one who is meditating; I am the devotee seeking the truth; I am the disciple of truth. To find out what the truth is, I have to detach myself from focusing my attention on the outer world of illusion, or appearances. As I focus on, and spontaneously follow the inhalation—the prana— the sound vibration is realized as hong. In that split second between inhalation and exhalation, and in that still point, we actually connect with the source, with the spirit within us—with that atman, or God—or with the core of existence, the root, or the essence. And as we exhale, the door to the infinite has been opened through the subconscious. In that moment of nonthought, or absence of thought, we enter the state of undifferentiated consciousness. I am neither this nor that: there is simply awareness. It is only a split second of experiencing pure awareness.

L.M.: Nonduality.

S. SHANK: Nonduality—I am aware that I am. That consciousness equates with the kingdom of God, the kingdom of all treasures. It is the kingdom of heaven that Jesus spoke of—as he was a practitioner of different meditation techniques.

L.M.: Do you think Jesus knew hamsa?

S. SHANK: Oh yes, definitely. It would have been unlikely that he had not known hamsa, considering that he did travel in India; and that he could have traveled quite a bit during the eighteen so-called hidden years between the ages of twelve and thirty.

L.M.: Now you believe that deeply, but the West doesn't believe this. We never hear about that in the teachings of the Christian church.

S. SHANK: There is a lot that the West has not heard about, including many saints and sages and sacred writings.

L.M.: There is a whole communion of saints of the East.

S. SHANK: That is a part of that spiritual heritage. There is, for instance, a whole tradition of Sivaite saints and Kashmiri saints. There are many ancient manuscripts and scrolls that are preserved in monasteries and ashrams in Tibet, Nepal, and India—that relate to this man of righteousness, this Isha, which means Jesus. There is even an Isha Upanishad.

L.M.: Do you think that is related to Jesus?

S. SHANK: No, not to him specifically. Though the name Jesus in Sanskrit is Isha, it corresponds to Isha. Jesus was exposed to various meditation techniques, and was qualified to practice them; he discovered the richness of those techniques.

L.M.: Do you think that he taught them to his closest disciples?

S. SHANK: I more than think so. I am self-persuaded that he initiated them into the light and into the sound—and into the mantrams, or at least some of them. There is a reference that supports that on the scriptural level, where he said: Let your consciousness be full of light. The mistranslation is: Let your body be full of light. It is not a mistranslation however, if we equate the body with consciousness; if we understand that symbolically and mystically, the body refers to the body of consciousness. The body contains within it all that is in seed form. So "let thine eye be single"—and your whole consciousness shall be full of light. How can these eyes become single? They don't. But it means your inner eye—which in Sanskrit is called *ajna*, or the spiritual eye. Let your eye be single: transcend dual vision, or dualism, and you will realize the light. Jesus pointed to man and said: "You are the light of the world." So, let your light shine. Well, it cannot shine forth if I am focusing on duality; if I focus on my limitations.

99

L.M.: That is darkness, metaphysically speaking.

S. SHANK: So long as that light doesn't shine, we are in darkness; and how great is that darkness. That is a metaphor for darkness, the darkness of ignorance. The mystics have always used these metaphors, and they all understand that language, regardless of which tradition they come from.

L.M.: The meditation you are presenting and teaching now is a continuation and honoring of that tradition. Though it is now much more accessible than in it was in previous times.

S. SHANK: I think so, because of the way my guru introduced the teachings.

L.M.: Who was your teacher?

S. SHANK: Swami Premananda. And in that guru lineage he received it from Swami Yogananda Paramahansa, who received it from Sri Yukteswar. And Yukteswar in turn was initiated into it by Lahiri Mahasaya. Lahiri was initiated into it.

L.M.: By Babaji.

S. SHANK: From Babaji, that is how it has come through this particular line of gurus. Now that doesn't mean that this is the only one line. Certainly, Babaji and all the others had other disciples, who in turn became gurus, and then initiated their disciples. Again, it was done by word of mouth. There is no way to calculate how many humans have received hamsa initiation throughout the ages. It has always been a secret tradition. My guru, Swami Premananda, always said: What is sacred is secret.

L.M.: We can't limit the creator, that absolute being, or that beloved, to any line of masters. Or say that, you must follow only this meditation because we are right, we have the only right teaching.

S. SHANK: I rejoice in the fact that it cannot be restricted to a few. It would be contrary to what I know to be God's nature—and, the nature of God's love.

100

One who loves unconditionally, does not limit that love to only a few. The same is true with these techniques. If these meditation techniques were lost, and did not continue to be taught by a guru line, I am certain that others would emerge. For when the need is great, the prayer is answered.

In a nutshell then, the philosophy of hamsa meditation—that the early revealers of it taught—is that hamsa means essentially this: I am *swa*, I am that. The realization came to the yogi that *swa* means that. I, the meditator, went into that—that for which there is no name. In our Vedantic tradition, God was not called God originally. God was simply called *tat*—t, a, t—that. The word God is a much later coinage.

L.M.: That thou art, say the Upanishads.

S. SHANK: That thou art: "*Tat tvam asi.*" Hamsa means I am that. In a circular way, as man continued meditating on that truth he came back to: I am that, hamsa, or I am swa—and, to swa: that I am. The emphasis had started shifting from I—the meditator who is going within, who is seeking the truth, and who is connecting with that—to the realization of that which I am meditating upon.

L.M.: That is really great.

S. SHANK: Exactly. Wow. Isn't it exciting and exhilirating? So that which I have been seeking, I am that. Moses had the same revelation when he went up to the mountaintop to ask God: God, what is your name? What do you hear in that question?

L.M.: I am who am.

S. SHANK: Why would he ask God, what is your name, if God had been the ultimate name—if Moses believed that God was indeed the name of God?

L.M.: It only points the way.

S. SHANK: Yes, yes; so he realized that what is called God in his tradition was not all of God. There had to be more to the identity of God. Now you remember that he had to remove his shoes: "Take off your shoes for the place whereon you stand is holy."

It's whole, it's perfect, it's sublime, it's pure; it's transcendent, it's divine. Only then was he able to approach the light. This is all of course a subjective dramatization of an internal process of revelation. What is your name?—that was his desire to know. The answer that came to him from within was: my name is I am. But I am what? Moses, or his mind, could not see that as a complete statement or revelation.

L.M.: It's beyond the conceptual mind.

S. SHANK: Yes, and so he asked what does that mean: I am—what? Is that all, I am? No, was God's reply, tell the people that "I am that I am." I am that hamsa—that I am. It is the same realization. Moses revealed the same truth. And surely, he initiated those who were qualified into that transcendental reality. A seemingly abstract, nonverbal reality that is nonspatial, nontemporal, nonphysical, nonsensory, and nonconceptual. It is without beginning and without end. So that is the basis of hamsa—and one who is initiated into it is taught exactly how to meditate on hamsa. There are many benefits that derive from this practice, physically, mentally, emotionally, and spiritually.

L.M.: When did you get initiated into hamsa?

S. SHANK: I was initiated by Swami Premananda. I was in college at the time, my sophomore year. I had been initiated into hamsa prior to that through Self-Realization Fellowship; I had taken their correspondence course, the lessons.

L.M.: When did you take the lessons?

S. SHANK: I took them the year before.

L.M.: Just the year before?

S. SHANK: I realized very early on that Swami Yogananda was guiding me. And just to pinpoint how he was: it was my senior year of high school, and I was in the public library. I was a prolific reader even then, but I had not found a book that spoke to my spiritual condition and need. One particular day, I was in the library, and suddenly, I felt something touch and nudge my foot.

A book was being pushed on my foot; and so I thought there must be someone on the other side. But there was no one there—there was no movement and there was no foot visible. So I bent down, and picked it up, and lo, and behold it was *Autobiography of a Yogi* by Yogananda.

L.M.: You had not heard of it before then?

S. SHANK: No, no, I had explored the Vedanta tradition, and was aware of Ramakrishna before that, but not Yogananda. I devoured the book from cover to cover.

L.M.: You felt the need for a living teacher.

S. SHANK: I knew that the guru would be paramount for my journey and growth. And that initiation into a meditation technique by an enlightened teacher was essential.

L.M.: A teacher you could talk and correspond with.

S. SHANK: I remembered seeing a picture in Yogananda's autobiography of another teacher, Swami Premananda, who was together with his guru Yogananda in front of the church in Washington, D.C. I began a correspondence with Swami Premananda; but I had to wait until the end of the summer to meet him. I'll never forget my first meeting with him, on that first Sunday in September. I knew at that moment that I had come home—and that I had met my spiritual teacher again. So he initiated me into hamsa; and then he gave me a second initiation into Om.

L.M.: What is the Om initiation?

S. SHANK: Om, or *aum*, is another very ancient Vedic mantram—it is the mantram of mantrams. Om is the word that was in the beginning, which the Gospel according to John talks about. It is the Greek *sphota*, or cosmic sound—and the *shabd*, or sound, in yoga. You will always find it at the beginning of the Upanishads and at the beginning of any chant. For instance, the Buddhists chant: "*Om mani padme hum.*"

L.M.: They do. So Om is the primordial sound.

S. SHANK: Exactly, it is the one out of which all other sounds have emerged.

L.M.: We have all emerged out of that Om.

S. SHANK: Yes, our form, all creation, everything: God spoke, and Om vibrated. So Om is given as the second level of initiation within the tradition.

L.M.: It is not quite as secret.

S. SHANK: Not quite as secret in that more information is readily available about the Om meditation technique. But the actual way of meditating on Om is also a secret tradition.

L.M.: You can find out practically anything about any spiritual path, and it has been said you can find all of the mantras, in books. But they are without the touch, and guiding presence, of the teacher.

S. SHANK: Yes, that is without the living touch. So even if the practice has been written down, it is not the same without that living touch and energy. The third technique is the kriya yoga meditation practice that is an integral part of our spiritual lineage and heritage all the way back to Babaji. Now you will find that there are some variations in the way kriya is taught, of what is taught by different teachers.

L.M.: Did you experience that with first SRF and then Swami Premananda?

S. SHANK: Yogananda adapted kriya to the Western lifestyle.

L.M.: That is very important.

S. SHANK: But Swami Haraharananda, the spiritual successor guru at Sri Yukteswar's ashram in India teaches an older form of kriya. It is very complex, very intensive, and time-consuming.

L.M.: That is more suited to the Indian temperament, and to the ashram environment.

S. SHANK: Precisely, when you live in an ashram, in that secluded environment, you are not commuting to work. Your life is rather well prescribed and ordered. It doesn't mean however that the spiritual benefits are greater because the practice is more complicated. Yogananda simplified it because if he had not, he would not have been able to reach the Western mentality, or connected with the Western way of living.

L.M.: He wouldn't have come to America at all.

S. SHANK: He is the teacher who brought kriya here in a simplified form, and which my guru Premananda also taught. This simplified technique allows anyone to practice it, even if they have physical limitations—the ancient form of kriya would exclude those people.

L.M.: Such as a handicapped individual. Now, the role of the guru on the spiritual path is exemplified by Jesus and Krishna, and Guru Nanak and Kabir; and by the Sant tradition in India. The guru's role is however much misunderstood in the West. How do you perceive the guru-disciple relationship—and do members of your Divine Life Church in Baltimore regard you as their guru?

S. SHANK: Yes, they do. I was accepted by many as the guru even before I officially became a swami, though I did not accept the title of guru. I kept telling them that I am not your guru, I'm not a guru. But they insisted, saying that whether or not you accept it, you are the guru to us. So I had to meditate long and hard about that over a period of years. Finally, I realized that if I were to continue to deny that guru-disciple relationship, what would that then say about my own relationship to the guru and the whole spiritual tradition?

L.M.: It is a kind of marriage between guru and disciple.

S. SHANK: I love the term marriage that you use. It is like a spiritual marriage, though I myself have never used that term. That is exactly what it is. The guru-disciple relationship is unlike any other human relationship.

L.M.: You found that as a disciple of Swami Premananda.

S. SHANK: Yes, and sometimes, the disciple sees the guru as a father figure. But I never did that.

L.M.: Some regard the guru as God.

S. SHANK: Or, God: no, it's not that. It is a spiritual marriage. And how do you communicate to someone the meaning and significance of a spiritual marriage, if they have no feeling for that?

L.M.: If they're not married.

S. SHANK: If they're not married, period. Even a human marriage is a reflection of that ideal, and has its roots, if you will, in a spiritual marriage. That can exist between a husband and wife without its being a spritual marriage, as in the guru-disciple relationship. In that relationship the disciple recognizes the guru as the guru—and the guru recognizes the disciple as the disciple. It is a spiritually ordained relationship. The guru is one who dispels the darkness by the light of illumination. The Bhagavad Gita says that the disciple is one who approaches the teacher with reverence, and right questioning, and humility. That is required of the disciple. So if that right attitude is not present, the guru will not accept that individual as a disciple.

L.M.: But we don't have to be perfect to be accepted as a disciple.

S. SHANK: Well, if we are perfect, then we are no longer the disciple, are we?

L.M.: Then we don't need to be the disciple. We are one with the One.

S. SHANK: Then we are not seeking anything further. Now, if I see that someone has a real yearning to know the truth, but is not familiar with the manner and approach that is called for, and, let us say, has some rough edges. I am sure that I had some of those when I met my guru. But what I did have is this reverence for the truth, this love of the truth. And yes, the guru looks into your heart, and it is the disposition of the heart that is the deciding factor, and not any external factors. Politeness is not a qualification, since it is not necessarily a good indicator of spiritual aspiration. Nor is sincerity. Someone may only want to impress you, and that will definitely be a barrier to forming the guru-disciple relationship.

The guru is concerned exclusively, totally, and completely with helping you to realize your goal, and with pointing out pitfalls that he, or she, has discovered on their own path and journey. And that they continue discovering: the journey is never over for the teacher as well. The guru-disciple relationship is cemented through initiation into a meditation practice. It will not flourish if the disciple does not honor the teachings and does not apply them diligently. The guru wants the disciple to realize that the supreme guru is within.

L.M.: Right, you point to the inner guru, that formless guru.

S. SHANK: That is my function, my purpose, my duty, my spiritual obligation. I will not allow anyone to worship the personality—that is anathema.

L.M.: That is never the way of true discipleship, or true guruship, for that matter.

S. SHANK: You can always know the true coin from the counterfeit. When the disciples asked Jesus: who are the false prophets, and how will we recognize them? He had urged them to beware of false prophets, or false gurus. How can we know the difference? Well, I had a little fun with that statement. I'm looking at, and saying, the word prophet: that sounds like profit. So, beware of false profits—that is, what are they after, what are the kind of payments they are asking of you?

L.M.: What's the material angle.

S. SHANK: What's the catch? So if these gurus promise you much, but tell you it will cost x amount. Then you shake the dust off your feet, bless them, and take to your heels as fast as you can. Secondly, any guru who is truly a guru will never belittle a disciple, and most assuredly, not in front of others.

L.M.: The true guru never puts down other teachers and other traditions.

S. SHANK: Never, never, never.

L.M.: It's what you found with Swami Premananda.

S. SHANK: The guru is uncompromising in his adherence to spiritual ethics and values. He will not compromise them for anyone, whether they are president or prima donna. The disciple's external status cannot, and should not, influence the spiritual relationship with the guru. There is an innate knowing and feeling of complete trust in the relationship. But the disciple may have some doubt or hesitation about committing himself to a particular guru—even when the guru is lauded as the guru of gurus, or the *satguru*—and is a very popular and charismatic guru. When the disciple does not feel that personal element—that his choice is based on a pure inner knowing—the relationship cannot flourish. It also continues for the mutual benefit of both. That is no sin if the disciple chooses to go his or her own way. There are those who would say it is a sin. I do not say it is a sin—if there is any sin, it is not remaining true to yourself.

L.M.: With the right teacher though, does the guru-disciple relationship continue even beyond death?

S. SHANK: That is an eternal relationship indeed. Now, Jesus came to John the Baptist with the express purpose that John should initiate Jesus. Baptism at that time actually meant initiation.

L.M.: It's the second birth.

S. SHANK: But John said to Jesus: I'm not worthy to do that. Jesus rather insists that John must do it: "for thus shall come the fulfillment of the law of righteousness." Jesus recognized that John had been his master, or guru, in a previous life. And John recognized that Jesus had since surpassed him in spiritual realization. Yet Jesus was honoring that eternal bond and was setting an example: that Jesus had already signed up with him for this guru-disciple relationship.

L.M.: The big boss sent me.

S. SHANK: Ordinarily we would think: Why would an avatar, a man of Jesus' stature, a savior—why would he have to be initiated? So there was his wisdom, and his humility was an expression of that.

L.M.: We need humility on the journey. It seems that we ought to have a sense of humor as well. What part does humor have amid life's continual ups and downs, and all the adversity and suffering?

S. SHANK: Humor is an indication of a good humor; it's a sign of a kindly spirit and disposition. Mahatma Gandhi once said something that has stayed with me for a long, long time, ever since I first read it. Gandhiji was interviewed by this reporter who had been following his work in India and South Africa.

L.M.: A Western reporter?

S. SHANK: He was either American or British. And he said: "Mister Gandhi, I have observed that you have such a tremendous sense of humor. How do you account for that, considering that you see so much suffering every day in your life"—millions of people starving, and in misery, and so on? Gandhiji replied: "Sir, if I did not have a sense of humor, I would have committed suicide long ago." You look at his life, and what he dealt with, and the issues and demands made on his time and energies. Yet, you see him constantly laughing about something, and smiling, and having a cheerful disposition. He cultivated that because he knew he was doing God's work, he knew that the truth works. He knew that the path of *ahimsa*, or nonviolence, and universal love brings an abundance of joy and well-being. I have not met a swami or guru who did not have a sense of humor, though it varies in degree. I have seen in my own journey that humor has always been a natural asset.

L.M.: It has assisted you on the journey.

S. SHANK: Oh, very much, and even more than humor, what has assisted me is my utter knowing that man is innately good. That life is innately sublime and good, and that life is really beautiful. That people are really, innately good. I don't mean good as compared with bad, that stands—but godly. I have met with so much of it in my life that the few pebbles of discordance I can count on my hand, compared to the countless ripples of joy, and love, and healing. I think humor is also very typical of—and, extending it now beyond the guru or swami designation—all humans of good will.

L.M.: Still I am led to think: Well, how much humor would I have if I had been one of the Jewish, or gay, or handicapped people on their way to Auschwitz—and, what about the slavery and inequality African-Americans have experienced—or what if I lived in Northern Ireland, or Bosnia, or Kosovo; or some other dangerous place? The list goes on. In short, why is there evil in the world? We can't just ignore that it exists, while we're on the spiritual journey.

S. SHANK: I don't dismiss that aspect of life. Though I see the totality of life, and I am mindful of both aspects of life. You refer to the condition of those in bondage, and any segment of society, or any individual, that suffers persecution. It's not that I stand-by and laugh, or find that funny at all. That moves me to compassion, that moves me to reflection. And that moves me to asking of my inner self to let me, or show me, how to be an instrument of healing to that individual, or persecuted group. It is true what the preacher Ecclesiastes says: that there is a season for everything. "A time to weep and time to laugh, a time to be born and a time to die"—he goes on in that vein. For me, that is the balance, the recognition, that pleasure and pain, joy and sorrow, loss and gain, that victory and defeat, faith and doubt, and hope and despair—all coexist. What we perceive as good and evil are really, as Buddha puts it, interrelative concepts; they are interrelated. Good and evil are both concepts that the human mind has conjured up.

L.M.: With disastrous consequences, at least on the physical, phenomenal level.

S. SHANK: We are giving power to certain phenomena that are neither good or bad in themselves. One brief example that we can certainly relate to is war. You mentioned Northern Ireland. I was traveling in the Irish republic and was advised not to go to the north. There were still skirmishes and attacks going on with shooting in the streets, and innocent little children and women had been killed. Now there is a history to that conflict. But these conflicts are not confined to Ireland. They have been repeated throughout history and in every country. So unless we gain a clear understanding of good and evil, we will continue to be emotionally biased. We must understand that good and evil are relative concepts—as seen from the Vedantic viewpoint. Vedanta says that good and evil exist so long as man believes in them. That which we call evil comes out of what hurts us. And that which gives us pleasure creates the concept of the good, or what is good. In the case of war, the people who attack us are described as the enemy, and being the enemy you are evil. Though in that scenario, in a war between two nations, who is not the enemy?

L.M.: There's always an enemy for each side.

S. SHANK: So both sides are at enmity with each other, and thus there is the idea of the enemy existing outside of us.

L.M.: What about the good life—and the good death? Meditation and the atmosphere of meditation we attempt to cultivate throughout the day will hopefully provide us with a clear understanding. And provide us with the chance to be partners with God in bringing the kingdom of heaven on earth. Then too we would study war no more.

S. SHANK: Meditation is very important, it is something that offers a cure or solution—that offers a tangible, viable, and powerful way for every human being to move beyond all relative concepts, such as good and evil. Now what all meditators have discovered through the ages is that they cannot get beyond the mind without meditation. This implies that there is something intrinsically wrong with the mind; that we have to overcome the mind to be at peace, or to be free. Not everyone, however, is in agreement with that perspective; and I am one of those people who isn't. That is because I recognize that the mind is like a mirror. So if you do not keep the mirror free of dust, what you perceive will be distorted.

L.M.: The mental mirror will be.

S. SHANK: When you accept your perceptions on the basis of this distorted image in the mirror as reality, you are left with judgment—one which is based on appearances, as perceived through a dusty lens. Our human experiences get interpreted in the fragmented and impure light of that dusty mirror. Man perceives the world with a dusty mirror. Saint Paul says in Corinthians:

Now we see, but through a glass darkly. This is due to our sensory impressions and value judgments about them.

Meditation essentially says that it is possible for us to see clearly—no matter which meditation technique, or mantram practice, we employ. The important thing is that all of them serve the same purpose—which is to help us push beyond the limits of the mind, the intellect, and the ego consciousness. Meditation helps us to reach that state of peace, calm, stillness, and balance. We finally can see clearly and also experience the totality of reality—that which is beyond the jurisdiction of the mind, senses, intellect, and all dualistic notions. There are those enlightened beings like Buddha, like Jesus, and like Krishna, Rama, Chaitanya, and Sankaracharya—who have moved through and overcome these barriers of the mind. Many of them choose to return from that state of bliss to speak and teach from their own experience. They avoid intellectualizing the truth. They know that you cannot realize the truth just by talking about it. But we can inspire someone to hunger for and persist in the search for the truth.

The idea of good and evil stops the moment you choose to drop all judgments. What are you left with when there is no judgment about anything or anyone? That nonreactive, nonjudgmental state allows you to deepen your meditation. And not to fear anything that comes up in your meditation. Now you no longer judge; you observe. You do not dwell on anything. You observe what would again limit you, or tempt you, to make a judgment.

Meditation is finally a very pure way of knowing that connects you with this stream of pure joy and bliss, and love, and freedom, and peace. The moment you experience that you want to go deeper and deeper. You are transformed on all levels, and you return with this influx of energy, consciousness, and stream of bliss. You are not experiencing the same level of consciousness that you had before you started the inner journey.

L.M.: Is meditation like death, like dying?

S. SHANK: Meditation is the willing, meditation is the process of discovering that you can never die. Meditation is finding out that death is the last grand and horrifying illusion.

L.M.: Yet most of us fear it so.

112

S. SHANK: The way we can help anyone who is afraid of death is to move through it. I know you have had many encounters with death, and with people around you, and those close to you dying, as I have. And I have never seen anyone not survive death.

L.M.: You mean the person who dies?

S. SHANK: I'm intentionally putting it that way. I have never seen anyone die. That means, I have never seen anyone not survive death.

L.M.: Then what is death?

S. SHANK: Death is the illusion; death is the barrier; death is the veil; and death is the partition between two rooms. It is creating the illusion that when we leave this room, or this body, now we are dead. Now we are no longer visible to the world. But death is nothing but the reemergence of that nonphysical reality, which is our greater self.

L.M.: Can we—should we—learn to enjoy death?

S. SHANK: Yes, if we can enjoy birth, then we can enjoy death. Because they are the same. To enjoy birth means to come consciously into this world. Very few have mastered that. Most of us experience the veil, or *maya*, coming down the minute that we enter the physical dimension.

L.M.: We experience the many, the world of duality.

S. SHANK: The Vedic statement of this is that the one becomes the many. To become, to experience the many, we have to let go of the remembrance of the one. Now Confucius said that he had long been perplexed by how most people weep when someone dies, and they rejoice when someone is born. He said the reverse should obtain. Because if you knew what lies ahead of you in this life, would you not have cause to weep? And if you knew that your sufferings were at an end when you die, would this not be a reason for rejoicing?

L.M.: It is all our attachment to things and to perceptions that bind us to the world. At death we get relinked with the eternal.

113

S. SHANK: Precisely, so what is there to grieve about? Krishna states it so beautifully and explicitly in the second chapter of the Bhagavad Gita. Arjuna is grieving about having to let go of his attachments for his family and former friends and teachers who are now his enemies.

L.M.: There is the war, he has to kill them.

S. SHANK: We see Arjuna's dilemma. Krishna tells him: Look, your grief is not based on the truth. It comes out of your attachment and the belief that you are going to kill somebody dear to you. Krishna enlightens him—and says that there is really nothing to grieve about—and that, the wise grieve neither for the dead nor the living. They know the truth about both of them is that the living will go on living; and the dead will go on living too. Can you imagine a stick that has only one end? But that is what we all do when we think of death as final. We think the stick has only one end.

L.M.: Now it's all over for me.

S. SHANK: There is only continuity, there is only movement, there is only the ongoing journey. You and I journey through this life from one state to another, or from one country to another. But we are still the same life force, or reality—we are still the same spirit or self or atman—we are still the same divinity or God-self. That we are—when we come into this physical manifestation. That we are—as we move through the waking state, the dream state, and the state of deep sleep. The state transcending the other three is the fourth one, or *turiya*—that transcendent, nonphysical state of consciousness.

We are in fact always alive, we are always unfolding, and we are always carrying with us the nature, and divinity, and qualities of that which man calls God. That reality which equates with consciousness, existence, bliss, and the absolute—*saccidananda*. So death is a blessing. Who would want to stay within the limitations of this physical instrument—or with a deteriorating and vacillating mind?

L.M.: Good point. No, we wouldn't.

S. SHANK: Exactly.

L.M.: Even though Methuselah may have lived nine hundred years.

S. SHANK: All right, if you live well. The key is to realize that we are immortal beings. That we are spiritual, immortal beings having mortal experiences. We are nonphysical beings having physical experiences—by choice. We are also beings who bring judgment into our life. And that is what creates misery.

L.M.: Judgment and desire.

S. SHANK: False desire, selfish desire. There is also desire in its pure state.

L.M.: Good desire.

S. SHANK: The desire for self-enlightenment, the desire to be an instrument of peace, and the desire to live in peace—the desire to grow in joy and wisdom, and love and understanding. That is a pure desire.

L.M.: Yes, right desire.

S. SHANK: And the desire to know the truth, the desire to be free—the desire to realize our oneness with all. Those are noble desires. You and I have the opportunity in our generation, in our time, to be an instrument of healing. Through right understanding, right realization, right service; through right livelihood, and through right sharing. By right, I mean what is in harmony with our inner being. It is possible in the midst of life's joy and sorrow to identify with that which promotes joy and reduces sorrow.

L.M.: Do you think that this way of meditation is at the root of all religions?

S. SHANK: I think that is where we are all at one, in terms of the different paths and religions. At the root of all the religions is the belief that man can have a better way of life than the one he is living now. That there is this one source of power, this one source called God, or it is called by various other names. And that is the source of our well-being.

Where the differences arise are in the means proposed by the various schools of thought, religions, and philosophies. This is where all the quarrelling occurs—concerning the ways and means to achieve bliss or reunion with God. All agree that we come from God.

115

Jain Meditation with Shree Chitrabhanu

L.M.: What is the role and importance of meditation in the Jain spiritual teachings? And what are the specific practices that are found in Jain meditation?

S.C.: The role of meditation in the Jain spiritual tradition is to lead our mind—and our perception—directly toward the self and one's essence. Through meditation we do these things. First, we relax. We drop—we let go of tension and stress. We clear the mental cobwebs, so that the mind becomes clean and clear. In that state we are balanced, we are at peace with ourselves. In that peaceful state, we see: what is the purpose of our life.

Why do we live? We eat, drink, and do one hundred things. But if we go on living for a hundred years, it is all repetition. Are we here only to repeat the same thing, day in and day out? So we try to become clear and a little serious, also. To see what is our role in this life, what is the purpose. And then, if we

116

are lucky we find some guidance to do this, which I call religion—that which helps to sustain us in our journey to excellence, to completion, to freedom.

Jainism is that idea. It is not any dogma. It is not a religion which tells you: we are superior, you are inferior; this is my religion, that is your religion. And if you don't follow my religion, you will go to hell. These negative thoughts do not find any room in the Jain teachings. Jain teaching is just a guidance in life; it's a nourishment—it sustains you. Because the journey is very tough, it is an uphill movement. So in that journey, we need something that sustains. Jain teaching is that sustenance, that substance, that energy; and that light that guides you.

It starts with reverence. In meditation, you come closer to yourself; for the first time, you have reverence for yourself. Yes, I am here alive; you feel the joy of being alive. That is the greatest thing: I am alive. Now everything is working. If I am dead, nothing matters. It may be a house, a church, a temple, or a million dollars. What have they do with a dead person? Now you are alive. So in meditation, you feel your breathing, your *prana*. Who takes the breath? The energy which is alive, which inhales and exhales. It takes oxygen inside, and throws out carbon dioxide, outside.

The oxygen is peace, love, positive thoughts—experiencing divinity within. Carbon dioxide is hate, jealousy, and greed. It is an ongoing process to make life alive; and to go on working every moment and every day. Because every moment, the vibrations from the world are coming at us. There are so many confused people, and they send their vibrations. We cannot escape from them. If we go on inhaling them, taking them in, we will feel confused. But through this purification process of inhalation and exhalation, we go on taking out carbon dixoide, those negative vibrations. We remain connected with the Jain teachings. And we take in those positive vibrations.

And for all of this, we need some model of behavior. Mahavira, the man, and Jain teacher for the present age—Mahavira is our model. He was born as a prince in the north of India some twenty-six hundred years ago, and he lived seventy-two years. Because of his previous lives, and all of his good merits at the time of his birth, he realized why I am here—the purpose of life. And he grew in this awareness. When the time came and his brother asked him to become the king, Mahavira replied: No, I am not here to rule over this people. I am going to fly, I am going to soar. I have not come to drag along on the earth and waste my years. I have to soar. He, Mahavira, was a human being. But slowly, slowly from the *atma*, he became *mahatma*; and from *mahatma*, he became *paramatma*. *Atma* means soul. *Mahatma* means great soul, like Mahatma Gandhi. *Paramatma* means the supreme. That is, you are upgrading yourself; the purpose of life is to upgrade, to evolve.

L.M.: That is the purpose of life. Not just to be bound to, attached to the false self, which is the typical, normal way we live.

S.C.: Yes, not to be bound. I have to live like a lotus flower. The lotus is in the water; it is in the mire, the mud. Still it keeps its head above that, and looks toward the sun, and opens its petals. So we live in the world with our family. But our heart is not in the *maya*. It is not in lust, not in hedonism. It is a beautiful feeling that I have to love humankind without condition. Accept others as they are, and not judge them. That is not my business. Because everybody comes with their own karmas. Your business is to perceive them as they really are.

L.M.: Do we have to begin by knowing ourselves first?

S.C.: Yes, yes, it starts with the self, and goes on expanding. That is the role of meditation. That meditation we call *dhyana*.

L.M.: Contemplation.

S.C.: Yes, and from it came Zen. And so, *dhyana* is—the first thing is—the mantra. When a meditator learns meditation, at that time a mantra is given: "*Namo arihantanam.*"

L.M.: And that means?

S.C.: *Namo* means I bow; *ari* means inner weaknesses, inner enemies. *Ari* has two or three meanings. The main meaning is enemy. Another is that your weaknesses are your enemies. They are within you.
Hantanam means destroyer, or remover. You are conquering your inner weakness. How do you conquer your inner weaknesses? By destroying them.

L.M.: How do you destroy them—is it a violence?

118

S.C.: No, it is not. Abraham Lincoln is said to have remarked, "I have destroyed all my enemies—by making them friends."

L.M.: Gandhi believed that too.

S.C.: Yes, that is the way. So what Mahavira did is, he removed and destroyed those weaknesses. The main ones are called *kashiya*—which is a group of four enemies, or weaknesses. One is anger; another is greed; the third one is the ego; and the fourth is deceit.

When you don't get what you want, you feel frustrated, and out of frustration anger comes. So first, one has to find out: Why am I creating expectation? Why do I not lead a simple life? To make a simple life for myself, I have to remove anger. How to remove anger? By being simple and peaceful. With peace and simplicity, you conquer anger. You make friends with peace and simplicity. Your life is simple. That is why a Jain monk won't wear ornaments and crowns and such. It is a very simple life. A saint is simple. So anger is removed.

Then comes greed. Greed is, we want everything. People's closets are full. But still they go to shopping centers; they want to buy more. There is no room in the closet now, but still they want to stuff it with more things.

L.M.: They probably never even wear any longer the things they already have.

S.C.: That is why even millionaires are unhappy. They don't have time to live life. There is no room for them. The room in our consciousness is cluttered with greed, with things. We are stuffing everything.

So meditation makes room. You must have room for yourself. Now you are cluttering yourself. When will you relax there in yourself? There is no room, you have bought up everything. The second is, again simplicity comes, contentment.

L.M.: Through meditation?

S.C.: Yes, you have to meditate on that—meditate on contentment. I am happy—the philosophy, or guiding principle, is that you become happy with whatever you get. And at the same time, you like to do what is imperative and necessary for you to do. In this way the second enemy, which is greed, is destroyed.

Then comes the third enemy, or weakness, which is the ego. We want to be superior to others. Meditation tells us: What is the connection between you and others? You are born at a different time, in a different place, and with different DNA. You have nothing to do with them. So why are you competing with others? It is your ignorance. You are competing with your own ignorance. Be what you are. And allow them to be what they are. So there is equality of all living beings. That is why in Jainism there is no caste system, no creed system. There is no question of man or woman—who is superior. Anybody can get *moksha*, anyone can get salvation.

L.M.: Be they a monk or a householder?

S.C.: Yes, anybody.

L.M.: There are no restrictions.

S.C.: No.

L.M.: Nobody has the inside track.

S.C.: You can be a *sannyasi*, you can be a *sadhu*; you can be a father, you can be a priest. But it is not that you have only to be that. So the third idea is to conquer or destroy this negative idea of ego.

The fourth is deceit. We see people who always camouflage whether they like somebody or not. When they meet you, they say: Oh, I'm glad to see you after a long time. But they think something else: Oh my God, why have I met him or her? So we are always playing, making a camouflage, or deceit. We are not honest with ourselves or others. Slowly, slowly, human beings have become a split personality; in this way, deceit creates a split personality. Thus, if one is not integrated within oneself, then one cannot achieve the goal—what he was meant to achieve. In order to achieve a goal, our purpose in life, one should be completely integrated.

L.M.: You can say one-pointed in a sense.

S.C.: One-pointed—there should not be a dichotomy between your belief and your behavior; belief and behavior must be integrated. There must be what is called the music of integration.

L.M.: We should be harmonious, and not full of cacophony, disharmony.

S.C.: That is the purpose. So these four enemies, you conquer them. And then the example, the model is there; you can see the beautiful statue here of Mahavira. Then I meditate, I say: I also can become peaceful, exactly like him. It is not his privilege alone. It is my privilege. We have a vision or thought of him in our meditation—in order to find our self. That my self is like that way of Mahavira: he is peaceful, with pleasant eyes, peaceful mind, and healthy body. And we allow the world to flow in its own way. So we build relations with the self, build relations with people; and we build relations with the universe, which is helping to sustain you. And don't do *himsa*, or violence, to anything.

Ahimsa is the first thing; it dawns in your mind. Ahimsa is, I want to be completely in tune with myself. And not hurt anybody. I always give, identify these six letters of the word *ahimsa*. The first letter *a*, is for appreciation. I appreciate myself. I appreciate being a human being, and having five good senses, and feeling well-being. I am alive. Then I say, I will be harmless, which is the *h* in *ahimsa*. Next is *i*—that I will have some kind of integration with whatever I do; with my words, with my actions, and with my thoughts.

L.M.: I suppose that extends to other creatures besides human beings as well?

S.C.: All, all—because we are supported by all, ecologically speaking. We are not alone. I wear clothes woven by somebody; my watch is made by somebody; my glasses are made by somebody; my food is made by somebody. How can I say my religion, my people—what is mine? You are supported by innumerable, invisible hands. That is why your connection is, or should be, harmonious with the universe. Any separation from them is a separation from yourself. So the third is integration, the *i* in *ahimsa*.

The fourth letter of *ahimsa* is *m,* for mastery. I have to master my impulses. I have to be a master of myself.

L.M.: Does that happen only very gradually? Or is it a lifetime's work?

121

s.c.: You go on working; it is not a one day's work. Someone asked me: How long do I have to meditate? I said: How long are you going to live? And he said, I am going to live a long time. So I say: meditate for a long time. If you want to live, it is like a breath.

l.m.: Meditation should be like our breathing.

s.c.: Once a day, you have time for yourself. Take out all the negative things—exhale. And inhale all the positive thoughts.

l.m.: Do you have a recommended amount of time for meditation practice?

s.c.: Yes.

l.m.: Is it one hour, or two hours, or what?

s.c.: No, I generally recommend twenty-four minutes and forty-eight, at the most.

l.m.: Why forty-eight minutes?

s.c.: Because twenty-four minutes would be for the twenty-four hours in a day. And so, you double that: forty-eight minutes. After that amount, the mind is not able to grasp more. It gets tired, exhausted. Whatever you do after that, you get fatigued. In school also, the period is usually forty-five minutes.

l.m.: Is posture important too, and should you sit in a comfortable—but erect—posture so that you don't fall asleep in meditation?

s.c.: You can select the posture which does not cause you to fall asleep. You keep aware; you can sit on a chair, or you can sit on the ground, or the floor. Make yourself comfortable. Because, right *asana*, or posture, is—must be—*sukhasana*, a posture which gives you comfort. It is not strenuous, or putting torture.

l.m.: On the body, that makes good sense.

s.c.: So in this way, you master your impulses and lower desires.

L.M.: Such as selfishness.

S.C.: And then, the *s* in *ahimsa* is service. You have to do something for others. You are taking so much service from the world. If you take something, you have to give something back. The main sutra of Mahavira says: "*Parasparo pagraho jivanam*"—*parasparo* is mutual; *pagraho* is help, and *jivanam* means life, or soul, or living being. It means that we are supported by each other. You have been supported, so you have also to support others. That is the *s* for service in ahimsa. And then, every day you advance somewhere, or make progress. The final *a* in *ahimsa* is for advance. So there are six steps in ahimsa.

L.M.: Sometimes though, you may not be aware of it, of your advancing, or making progress in a given day?

S.C.: But you are living a good life. For example, you are sitting on a train. You are not aware that it is moving; but you have taken the right direction, right train, and you are moving.

L.M.: It is just like meditation.

S.C.: Because the spring comes and the flower blossoms. They blossom by themselves. You have not to ask the flower to bloom. It is the presence of the spring, that is all.

L.M.: Historically, the Jain religion seems to have been concentrated primarily in India and Asia.

S.C.: Yes.

L.M.: But today, and especially over the last twenty-five years, Jainism has been having a lasting impact on America and the West. You are definitely playing a big part in all of this. How do we understand this important development and growth of Jainism in America and the West?

S.C.: What happened was, before that time no Jain monk had come to teach here. And so, among scholars who were talking and writing about

Jainism, there was only a kind of half—a partial understanding. But in 1970, when I transcended my traditional monastic limitation.

L.M.: A new Jain era began. As a longtime Jain monk you couldn't travel, you were forbidden to.

S.C.: I went to Geneva, Switzerland. It was the second spiritual summit conference in Geneva. The dean of Harvard who also attended the conference met me. I was the main speaker representing ahimsa, and the Jain teaching of *anekantavada*, or the relativity of thinking.

The Harvard dean was very much impressed by the ideas of the reverence for life, nonviolence or ahimsa, and of the relativity of thinking. He told me we are going to hold the third spiritual conference at Harvard, in 1971. And he asked me, would you like to come to America? I was elated, because that was my dream, to go to Harvard. So I hugged him and said: Sir, you are very good. I was speaking from my heart. So I came here. At that time, Jains were not many. Some students from India were here who were studying in college.

L.M.: They were mainly Indians?

S.C.: Indians, but they also were boys, youth. How can someone know anything much about Jainism if there was no teacher and no Jain temple? Meantime, I stayed in a hotel for a month, and was received with a group of people by the governor.

L.M.: The governor of Massachusetts.

S.C.: And then I gave a talk, and the *Boston Globe* wrote something about me. So many people were attracted to this teaching.

L.M.: Many Americans?

S.C.: Yes, Americans—that is because Americans are always open to something new. They are smart; though sometimes they are brainwashed by TV and the media. Some Americans came, and then they asked me to stay longer. So I decided to stay, but there was no place.

124

L.M.: There was no place for you to meet.

S.C.: Then an American lady, her name was Elizabeth Cattell, she opened her house to us. She said, you can come to New York. She was an old lady, a very good person; she was a Quaker. Thus, my wife, Pramodaji, and I stayed some fifteen months in her house. She did not charge any rent. And she began to follow my teachings. Later on, she wrote a book about me. During that time, I got an invitation to teach Oriental philosophy at the State University of New York college in Purchase. I accepted that because I wanted to earn a living here in America. I cannot live on alms here. In India, I was living on alms.

Then in 1973 I opened a meditation center in Manhattan on Eighty-sixth street. My students rented that place and I was teaching meditation there. It started off very slowly. The first Jain temple we had was in our meditation center; now it is in Queens. Then I decided to spread the Jain message. A former church in Boston was turned into a temple. Also, in New Jersey and in Toronto, we turned former churches into temples. And later we moved into a very big building in Toronto. In this way, the journey started in 1971. And now, about 80,000 Jains belong to our JAINA organization.

L.M.: Is that only in the U.S.?

S.C.: We call it JAINA, which means Jain Associations in North America.

L.M.: So the U.S. and Canada together have 80,000 members? That's very impressive.

S.C.: There are fifty-seven centers now. So Jainism is taking flight, Jainism is everywhere now. But not as a religion. It is the idea of reverence for life—it is a way of living. That is why it has become famous. Now I am arranging a children's program. It began in 1996. The first time, two hundred boys and girls stayed together for three days in Chicago. In 1997, there were six hundred boys and girls.

L.M.: It was a retreat for youth with you?

S.C.: The boys and girls are over sixteen but under thirty-five years of age. They have an organization called YJA or Young Jains of America. The third meeting took place in 1998, in Houston over the 4th of July. There were over seven hundred boys and girls. They made the commitment that they will practice nonviolence; that they will represent a reverence for life; and that they will conduct themselves ethically and morally in life and in business. There are MBAs, MDs, and lawyers who have all started the movement. So in these years, the dream that I had has become a reality.

L.M.: Back when you were in India, you had this dream to come to America.

S.C.: Yes, yes, I thought the Western world has a great material capacity. It is able to reach the moon. But they are also fighting, and having violence in their society. If they don't have reverence for life, they will use guns to kill their own neighbors, their own people. I had a dream to talk to people in the United Nations. Though I did not have this vast dream all at once, how it would come out. It turns out to be a very big dream now—beyond my first dream.

L.M.: You must be doing the right kind of dreaming, as Jainism is doing so well here. Now what is the good life? And how does this practice of ahimsa, along with the Jain emphasis on vegetarianism—how does this contribute to better living—environmentally, socially, and for the individual?

S.C.: Once you begin to live a life with integration, that life itself is a good life. It is not that something good is different. When you are harmonious in your behavior and with your belief, that is a good life. Your behavior and belief are—have—reverence for life. First, you have to have reverence for yourself. I will not do something that puts me down in my own eyes. When I am alone, I should not feel down about myself that I say: My God, what a messy man I am. Rather, I feel that I am clean—so one has to feel good with oneself. If something is wrong with us, we do not have to identify with that. We have to talk with ourself: "That it is a condition, it is not me. I am pure consciousness, I am divine, I am evolving." The philosophy of evolution states that we started from lower than ameoba; and now we have become a human being. So in each life, by burning karma—and through suffering and through service—we are evolving. We were in tree life, and in animal life, but we have evolved. Though some residue of animal life we still have. Sometimes, we are like a dog, we bark; sometimes we are like a fox, we are very cunning; and, sometimes we are like the cobra, we become angry. So we have some residue of that.

126

L.M.: Definitely, it does seem that way.

S.C.: But we are evolving.

L.M.: The Jain teachings are fairly unique in advising that all followers should be vegetarian.

S.C.: That is why I think it shall be a sustaining idea for the twenty-first century. For those who want to excel themselves in the journey to perfection and excellence, this must be something positive. Jainism has no violence, or negativity. It does not believe in any dogma—in the name of religion. I am not very religious. Religion has done a lot of wars, killing, and judgment. They have burned people alive in the name of religion, such as Joan of Arc. And people now go on discriminating that: You are this, or you are that. The moment religion comes, we separate each other.

So I don't believe in religion. With Jainism, it's a beautiful idea that you practice. I don't think there is any need to be dogmatic. I don't ask anybody to become a Jain, because to convert someone is an act of physical violence. You are forcing somebody with your ideas. But life is life. Let it understand what is good for it, what is healthy for it. The three stages of life are: the animal, which wants to good; the human being, who wants to do good; and the divine, who wants to be good. So we become good—that is divinity. Not, we want to do good; that is human endeavor. If you are good, whatever you do will be good.

L.M.: It is your own nature, that you have found that.

S.C.: The sun is light, so it gives light. The flower is fragrant, so it gives you fragrance.

L.M.: Doing naturally what its nature is.

S.C.: So then, go to your nature. But sometimes we appear bad. That is because of our conditions, our conditioning. Not because of our nature. It may be a condition of karma; a condition of the past life; a condition of the parents, or a condition of society. We are nothing but a product of the various conditions. Still, we do know of another way. When we find it, we can slowly break these many conditions.

L.M.: We can through meditation and service.

S.C.: Meditation, yes. And Mahavira is a good example for us.

L.M.: How long ago did the first Jain teacher live?

S.C.: Adi was the first, beginning thousands, perhaps millions, of years ago. Adi means Adamlike. Then, the teacher Parshwanath lived about 850 B.C. And Mahavira lived around 599 B.C.

L.M.: That is very close to the Buddha's time.

S.C.: The Buddha was later on. And also, for seven years, Buddha practiced asceticism.

L.M.: In his growth, on his path toward becoming Buddha?

S.C.: In the beginning—Buddha came from Nepal. And he came to Magadha where Mahavira had lived, which is around Patna, in Bihar. So Buddha practiced Shramana for seven years. But then, he found it a little too ascetic. So he selected the middle path.

L.M.: I didn't know that. Now you've said that Jain meditation can be practiced equally well, whether you decide to be a monk or nun, and live in a monastery.

S.C.: Yes.

L.M.: Or, you can have a family life, in the world.

S.C.: Yes.

L.M.: What is the understanding of a living teacher, such as yourself? And what is the Jain view of the guru? It is difficult for most of us to recognize who is the right teacher. One who will guide us to what is called right vision.

S.C.: It is a very difficult thing. If you want to buy a diamond, you have to take time to understand who is a right jeweler, one who does not cheat you.

L.M.: Right, someone knowledgeable and honest.

S.C.: You have to take time. Then also, you learn what a real diamond is. The Bangkok stone sparkles like a diamond; the Hong Kong diamond, also—it is a sparkling stone, it is not a real diamond. So there are many people who come as the guru. But what is their actual achievement in so many years? You are giving your life to them; you are getting guidance from them. So searching for the right teacher is more important than searching for the right diamond.

When you see the attitude of reverence in a teacher—his approach, his simplicity—and that way of living. Then that teacher guides you, because he is practicing reverence. Some people say: thou shalt not kill. But if, when he takes lunch, he devours animals; that cannot be a good teacher. What he was talking about just now in the pulpit is different from what he is now doing.

Do not be in a hurry to take a guru. Take time to find out the right person for you on your journey. The guru is he or she who removes the darkness of your ignorance. *Gu* means darkness; *ru* means remove. He helps you ultimately to find your own inner guru. And the guru gradually disappears—you become your own guru.

L.M.: Does the teacher recognize his students?

S.C.: We are all students. Even the guru sometimes realizes that: I am also a student. He should not go on an ego trip, that I am the guru. The moment he feels that I am completely the guru, he is no longer guru.

L.M.: The guru is always learning too.

S.C.: Yes, yes, he is learning from the higher level. And then, he is imparting that knowledge to the seekers.

L.M.: It is really free and belongs to the universe.

S.C.: To the universe, yes—that guide we need in life. Life is surrounded by so many things. There are so many temptations. There is so much brainwashing. There are so many types of subliminal suggestions, and so many of our conditions, also. We need someone along the journey of life who can give us some glimpse, who can be a role model for us.

L.M.: During Jain meditation, does the student visualize the form of the teacher, Mahavira?

S.C.: Sure, yes.

L.M.: That is part of the *dhyana* or contemplation. Do many Jains also have a shrine like the one you have here?

S.C.: Yes, a smaller version.

L.M.: Of course it's not the physical object one meditates on, but on the reality which the image points us to?

S.C.: It is not the object. It is inspiring, it is the inspiration.

L.M.: People don't worship statues in Catholic churches, they are only reminders of that truth.

S.C.: Yes, that is the truth. But people get carried away in their worship; and they forget that they have to live like that.

L.M.: As those great Jain figures did. Still we can't just leave it up to them. It has to be realized by us now.

S.C.: Yes.

L.M.: Right now, there is a pressing need for spiritual community. Especially here in the West where we seem to have so little sense of community at all. The need is greater than ever in this materialistic society. How do we build more spiritual community with each other?

S.C.: Light likes the light. And it is ongoing light. So, there must be right vision. One makes the commitment that, from this day on, my life will not be hurtful to myself. I will not smoke, which leads to cancer. I will not drink, which pollutes my mind. I will not take meat, as killing hurts my purity. I don't want to cause pain to any living thing, such as by wearing fur or silk, or animal products, or cosmetics which cause suffering.

L.M.: That require experiments on animals.

S.C.: This way one is practicing reverence for life in one's own life—be it in eating, in wearing clothes, in doing business, and in earning one's own living. Then too you are inspiring another person who comes in touch with you. It may be your wife, it may be your husband; it may be your child, it may be your neighbor. The American government has passed a law that Jains are free from any future military draft. Jains are not able to kill human beings. They cannot even kill a chicken.

L.M.: They can't even serve in the military.

S.C.: They will never serve because they are useless. They are not able to kill.

L.M.: We should all be so useless.

S.C.: Then you don't need war.

L.M.: No, we don't. Death however stands out as an event in our lives that is filled with mystery to some degree. Many of us also experience some fear over the question of death, our own death.

S.C.: Death is, once you go deep down into yourself. Ultimately, you realize that you have taken the body to complete this mission. Whatever is left out, left unfinished, you will take another body to finish. And also, what you have done in this life will result in the next life. So my life has not been given to me by God, or somebody else. What I have done previously—according to that, I got my parents and my life. What you sow, that you reap. If you plant a mango tree, a mango comes; if you plant a bitter lemon tree, a bitter lemon comes. Karma is nothing but what we do with thoughts, words, and actions. It is the result of our actions. I call it consequence. Life is nothing but a consequence of what we have done.

L.M.: Does that fit in with what you were saying about the teaching of relativity?

S.C.: Relativity means seeing the same point from many angles. It is also called karma, it is rebirth. Your next birth will be according to the life you live now.

L.M.: Though it's not necessarily in the physical dimension. Could it be a rebirth in an astral, or causal, or other body?

S.C.: Anywhere, the whole universe is a very vast cosmic entity.

L.M.: You would apply the relativity principle toward one's experience of death. We shouldn't fear it.

S.C.: Whether you fear it or not, what is going to come is going to come. So why not accept it joyfully?

L.M.: We don't like suffering.

S.C.: If you go on being fearful, fear causes the suffering. When we grow old, the ears cannot hear, so we go to the doctor; the eyes cannot see, so we go to see doctors, and they operate. Our body is not well, we always have to take injections. The joints may have pain. The body is not able to function as when we were young. And at that time, death gives you liberation. Then, you discard this old car.

L.M.: We're glad to be leaving the old, worn out body.

S.C.: You'll have a new car. Because you led a good life, it will be better than the one you have now. We have already evolved from the past life. Jainism means the evolution of consciousness. The body is just a form to go on evolving with.

L.M.: Through death, is there a God, or divinity, that we see, that we experience?

S.C.: First of all, Jainism teaches that your own self is the hidden God. That the kingdom of God is within you.

L.M.: As Jesus said.

S.C.: Everybody says that, you have to say that. And that, you are the God. God is not outside. Bernard Shaw says: Beware of those whose God is in heaven.

L.M.: The famous playwright.

S.C.: George Bernard Shaw—he said, they don't see God in life. They only see God in church, or in heaven. But no, God does not live in walls. God lives in life. So ultimately, as we purify, we are coming closer to God. Complete fullness of goodness is Godhood—goodness in full bloom is Godhood.

L.M.: A perpetual spring, always spring. Then suffering has a purifying role.

S.C.: Yes.

L.M.: At the present time, there is still a lot of competition among the different religious traditions. Keeping in mind your own personal experiences with interreligious dialogue here in America, what do you think are the prospects for the religions working together for the benefit of humanity, and indeed for all creation?

S.C.: If we unite, we will unite through feeling love and reverence. Not through religion. Religion will not unite us. Religion often starts as a new movement. It is a kind of shop, a new religion is open.

Someone will say: Why don't you join my shop? The religions are the different shops in the name of God. Everybody is selling the commodity of God. They sell their own concept, their own belief. And the moment a person leaves the religion, they will say he is an atheist. One Catholic priest who is in an important position in the church said to me: If I give this up, then they will take away my collar.

L.M.: If he left his position in the hierarchy?

S.C.: If he left his Catholic belief. He told me that then the people will not believe in him, they will not follow him. I don't want to be lonely at this age. I am not able to take such an adventurous step as you have taken. He is a very wise man. So his feeling was, if the religious person gives up his religion, his shop will be closed. Then he is not being loyal to his own Christianity. Or he is not loyal to his Judaism; or he is not loyal to his Hinduism. And if I were such a religious person, they would say that I am not loyal to Jainism.

But I say, I am not here to propagate religion. I am here to give ideas which are healthy and wholesome for humankind. So, unite in the name of love. And let love unite us. We are the creatures of love, we are born from love. And if you want to make a very materialistic statement, when our parents were making love, then we were born. So if we have the spiritual love, divine love, unconditional love, we will unite.

And I am hopeful that the day will come when people will unite in the name of ahimsa, reverence for life; caring for the earth; caring for our environment; caring for life; and caring for the suffering of animals. If we go that level, we will unite. But if we are on the ideological level, it is difficult. I am not against anything. But it is very difficult that way.

L.M.: There is a blind attachment to these religious traditions.

S.C.: Yes, it is a big attachment; it is like your skin. It is not changing your shirt, it is taking off your skin. A condition is like your skin.

L.M.: You don't teach a Jainism that is sectarian or dogmatic. Now what if one thinks: This is it, I'm ready and convinced that I want to follow the Jain teachings—what do I have to believe as a Jain?

S.C.: You have to believe in mainly three things. One is, that Mahavira is the purest example. You are meditating, and you say: that evolved state is my state of consciousness. Forget about the name, the name Mahavira is an example, a model. The second thing is that I am soul, I can evolve and reach that state. Believe in your complete evolution. And nobody is going to help me. I have to help myself, I have to evolve. And then, whatever I do, it has a consequence. There is no sin, no punishment. If I eat good food, I will be healthy. If I eat junk food, I will be sick. So if you lead a peaceful life, you will have peace. If you have a crazy life, then you will be crazy.

Again, the three essential things are: right knowledge; right vision; and right character. Right vision means that you want to be completely peaceful, as Mahavira has preached. That is right vision. Right knowledge means that you are soul. You are evolving, and you are having a relation with the universe. And the third is right character. There is harmony between your behavior and your belief, an integration of that. If we have, or take, these three steps in our life—we will be able to make our life very meaningful. At the same time, it will be joyful. We will celebrate that, yes, I have made my life very meaningful. Now my time has come: goodbye. Whatever is left out, undone, I will resume when I am reborn. You have a belief in your rebirth, and in your immortality. You don't see yourself as a failure. You have read the *Song of Life*, which was written by Longfellow. He says: "Life is real, life is earnest. And the grave is not the goal." It is the goal for the body—not for the soul.

L.M.: So we could say love is that goal. Love is that gospel. It is the goal of the meditation that one practices, and the service one renders. All of those things should be done with an attitude of reverence, a love for life. That brings us there.

S.C.: With meditation, first you relax. Then you calm down. You clean your slate and take out the mental cobwebs. And then you ask: Who am I, who am I? You say well, I am me, I am myself. But before the name, who was I? I was energy. Actually, I am indestructible energy. And when you get that glimpse, you stay with it. I must use this energy which takes me toward goodness, takes me toward reverence.

Whatever I do, my doing should be done with reverence. I eat, drink, talk, and meet others. There is no need to collect hate. If other people are not good, let them be bad then. You allow them to be in their place. And respect yourself. So that you don't take that negativity home with you. Or else, then you become a victim of their bad influence.

L.M.: You are an actor, not a reactor, in life.

S.C.: Yes, an actor. I call it a witness. You are witnessing. You go to a movie and watch all kinds of dramas. But you are sitting there—you witness. So, let it go. And whatsoever you like, you take that home. You think: Oh, that was the good part in the movie.

CHRISTIAN SANNYASA WITH WAYNE TEASDALE

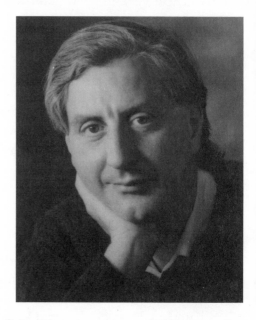

L.M.: What is the meditative way of the Christian sannyasi? What are the chief characteristics of the sannyasic life? One of the great modern exemplars of the Christian sannyasic path has been Dom Bede Griffiths, who initiated you into sannyasa.

W.T.: Sannyasa itself is the mystical path—and it is the complete commitment to the mystical life. It has as its focus and center the dropping of—and detachment from—everything. Going in search of the divine—the Absolute, or the Godhead, sannyasa finds a resonance in Christ's words: "If you will be perfect, go and sell what you have, give your money to the poor, and come follow me." Well, come follow me is to do the work of the kingdom. But it is also to seek intimacy with the divine. That is what the sannyasi does. Since the divine is infinite, it overflows all our categories, all our labels—and all of our neat divisions into different religions. The sannyasi, or the renunciate—

and sannyasin is the female—is beyond religion, is beyond dogma, is beyond doctrine—and is beyond all theological formulations. God is always infinitely more than that, no matter what tradition one comes out of.

L.M.: Sannyasa does not initally come out of the Christian tradition. It is not limited to the Christian tradition.

W.T.: Yes, a sannyasi is a sannyasi. Most of them are Hindus, some may be Buddhists and some are Christians—each one of them with their respective culture, background, identity, and tradition. Being a Christian sannyasi, I think what characterizes it is this quest for contemplative experience, and to live the intense mystical life. For the Christian sannyasi, there are the demands of the gospel, and the demands of love, that are very profound.

In their seeking the divine and being a fully formed contemplative mystic, the Christian sannyasi is always available to the demands of compassion, love, service, kindness, and mercy; and to the demands of prophetic witness and sticking one's neck out for justice. The sannyasi makes an absolute commitment to spiritual practice and to a life of simplicity—what we call poverty in the Christian tradition. There is an absolute commitment to love and mercy, and kindness and sensitivity; there is a commitment to awareness—to an ever-expanding awareness. A sannyasi seeks a closeness to creation and nature that includes an attitude of reverence, and being a healing presence to other species.

L.M.: Nature is sacred, and all sentient beings.

W.T.: Nature is sacred, all sentient beings are sacred. Sannyasa brings an attitude of nonharming; and also an attitude of the preciousness of all of this—and one's active communion with creation. The sannyasi works to break down the barriers that separate religions, cultures, peoples, and nations. A sannyasi must be fundamentally rooted in dialogue with them.

L.M.: They are almost a kind of messenger.

W.T.: They are messengers of the transcendent dimension, the sacred dimension.

L.M.: How has sannyasa evolved? Christian sannyasa is not such an ancient tradition. Did sannyasa begin with the Vedas?

W.T.: Sannyasa is a medieval Sanskrit term within the Hindu tradition. There are fifty or so terms in Sanskrit for the renunciate, the ascetic, or mystic sage. No, I don't believe it began with the Vedas.

L.M.: With the Bhagavad Gita, then?

W.T.: This reality of the ascetical, mystical life of the *rishi* or mystic seer began thousands of years before the Vedas.

L.M.: Before the Vedas?

W.T.: It is beyond the Vedas—a conservative estimate is that it's at least seven thousand years old. Probably it's more realistic to say that it's fifty thousand years old.

L.M.: Perhaps even as old as the primal, aboriginal religions?

W.T.: Exactly, it's really the primordial monasticism.

L.M.: Might aboriginal peoples have a form of sannyasa without their specifically calling it that?

W.T.: I would think so, because they certainly have the experience of the divine. We now know that there has been a religious consciousness on our planet for 500,000 years. The religions themselves are the new kids on the block.

L.M.: I am not familiar with that. Who has cited that number?

W.T.: Hans Küng has talked a lot about it.

L.M.: All right, 500,000 years. Now I do know that your own association with Bede Griffiths—and his being a Christian sannyasi—are central to contemporary Christian sannyasa.

W.T.: Regarding the history of Christian sannyasa, the first Christian sannyasi was Roberto De Nobili, who was one of the Jesuits in India, in the late 1700s. That was when the movement began, though it became dormant for a while. There was a lot of antagonism to the inculturation that De Nobili represented from the Portugese Catholic hierarchy in India, who were very conservative. And so, they had to subvert it.

L.M.: Did De Nobili take sannyasa initiation from a Hindu teacher or guru?

W.T.: I'm not sure of that, I don't think so. Though this innovation was approved by the Pope; the Jesuits are always way ahead in these things.

L.M.: As with Matteo Ricci in China, his attempts at integrating Chinese religion and philosophy with Christianity—which Rome eventually rejected.

W.T.: I suspect that there have been Christians taking sannyasa for hundreds of years before that. There is the mention of Saint Thomas, the apostle, going to India in the first century, in a letter of the Greek father Hippolytus. I think that so long as Christians have been going to India, there have been these spiritual geniuses who were ahead of their time, like Henri Le Saux or Abishiktananda.

L.M.: That's in the second half of the twentieth century. And Le Saux was from France?

W.T.: He was a French Benedictine monk. There are probably a lot of others too, brave pioneer souls who maybe lived a very hidden holiness within sannyasa, and are not known at all.

L.M.: Those who didn't write, or publish, about it. Abishiktananda apparently met Ramana Maharshi. Did he perhaps take initiation from the Hindu Swami Gayanananda?

W.T.: He may have taken initiation. There was also the priest Jules Mochanin, who was a very holy man and who co-founded Shantivanam ashram with Abishiktananda. The intent was to be totally Indian and totally Christian at the same time.

L.M.: Please describe now your own meditation practice, and discuss its importance for your life within this Christian sannyasa tradition.

W.T.: My spiritual practice very much centers on meditation—contemplative prayer, or contemplative meditation. I like to say contemplative meditation rather than Christian meditation—contemplative meditation instead of Centering Prayer. There is only one meditation—just as there is only one sannyasa. Though there are people from different traditions who take sannyasa. There is only one consciousness. And there is only one love; all love is the same. There are different expressions of it, but love is love. Then too to have compassion is to let go of yourself. Now I prefer to use the term contemplative meditation because that is the goal. It is contemplative, mystical experience that is a direct kind of contact with the divine—through being receptive to the divine presence. An important distinction between Catholics, or Christians, in the West and Indians is—the Indians will never ask you: What is your idea of God? They will ask you: What is your experience of God?

So it's out of this experience that I am speaking. I have always known it to be a personal, intimate, enveloping, invading, and irruptive, divine presence. But it is very apophatic, because you never see God's face. I remember something Bede said to me one day many years ago, while on a walk in a London park. We were talking about the nature of mystical experience, and of contemplative mystical union. And he said to me: "It's like sitting in a dark room." This is the *via negativa*. You are sitting in a dark room and someone comes in. You can't see them. And they put their arms around you. You know they're there. But you can't see their face.

You have this incredible intimacy with God, but there's always mystery. You know it as this incredible, loving, all-embracing and all-consuming presence. That is my experience of God, and I think that my awareness is maintained through the grace of God. It's not anything that I am doing. I always kind of consider myself to be a failure at meditation.

L.M.: I know I do, maybe we all think that.

W.T.: I have been trained as a philosopher and theologian, and one of the great hazards of that is having a mind.

L.M.: A too analytical mind.

140

W.T.: Presumably we all think, and that is very useful in so many areas of life—except prayer.

L.M.: We are too calculating.

W.T.: We're calculating, but where you don't need that is in contemplative prayer.

L.M.: Whether it's in making human love—or, in our experiencing divine love—that won't work.

W.T.: It won't work. In fact, it can't work there. In active contemplation, there is the part that is my effort—which is united with grace. And in this relating to God—intimacy with God—I feel so often a failure. Yet I also experience constantly the divine making up for my deficiencies in prayer by carrying me through it. One way in which the spirit carries me through prayer—and carries me along in my life—is through the grace of being aware of the spirit's presence.

L.M.: Some mystical poets like John of the Cross use the language of sexual love to evoke spiritual love, the mystical union of the soul and God. It is all one and the same energy.

W.T.: It is one energy, but it's used differently.

L.M.: Is the concentration practice that you use in your meditation similar to concentrating at the third eye, or the *kundalini* practice found in yoga?

W.T.: I have done that. But as I say, I am very much a failure at meditation. And so I have just surrendered to the divine presence. I am aware of it, I experience it constantly—not simply in prayer, but most of the time. If I allow myself to be aware of it, it's there. It is just a question of removing the obstacles to your awareness. It's God's grace, it's not me. I can't make it happen; it just happens. All I can do is go back to my room and make myself receptive.

L.M.: That's a key word, receptive. The Christian sannyasi's meditation practice is not like discursive prayer. It is listening, more than anything else. Isn't it really a kind of waiting?

W.T.: It is waiting, and waiting, and waiting. Meditation is complete mindfulness of that reality—a conscious seeking of and aspiring to it. My spiritual practice is in many ways the most important activity of my life. It is not more important than love, and mercy, and compassion. But it is really the basis, or foundation, for me to be compassionate. I think that it all works together; and all of it is the fruit of that connection with God.

L.M.: That's right, if you really love someone, you just want to be with them.

W.T.: You want to be them.

L.M.: And you want to be present to them?

W.T.: Exactly.

L.M.: Even if we can't, as you've said, see them. What you say about being a failure is a relief to me. Most meditators may be alike in that regard. Is it that there isn't such a great gap between the sannyasi's meditation, and the lay person's meditation, after all?

W.T.: That is just a label. Existentially, all these distinctions of clerical, or priest, or lay person don't mean very much.

L.M.: Yet we're caught up in them.

W.T.: To God, it means absolutely nothing: God does not see those distinctions, and does not respect them. All that God cares about is the heart, where one's heart is. And what are you doing to the least of my brethren? Not what are you called, what degrees, or how much money do you have, who do you know. These things mean nothing to God. And when you did it to the least of my brethren, you did it to me. Can what we do lead to *moksha*—or liberation—or nirvana?

L.M.: Is that actually?

W.T.: The goal.

L.M.: That's not to say that you deliberately think that when you meditate. Rather it's unexpected, it's a gift.

W.T.: Yes, it is a gift. What does liberation really mean? Moksha, or nirvana, is not all the lights, and flashes, and illuminations. It is a movement of your will in which you let go of your desires; it is when you let go of your selfishness. When you're not self-centered, and fixated on your self all the time.

Bede once made a statement concerning the nature of sanctity that would today sound very Buddhist; though it is really very Christian. He said that sanctity, or holiness, is being very much aware of how we are conditioned by the ego—of how much our ego-self is a problem. It is a problem for everyone. But to be aware of it as the problem is half the battle. Holiness is being aware; holiness does not mean that you don't have an ego. And that you don't allow the ego to get in the way of love and compassion. That you're able to set the ego aside, and respond to others.

L.M.: It's learning to act.

W.T.: You cannot kill it though. I mean, you cannot emasculate your being. You have to integrate everything.

L.M.: Religion has led us to believe that being religious means an emasculation, almost a castration of the person.

W.T.: Actually, it is also denying your body. The rejection of the body which so epitomizes Christian monasticism was once put into the neat little aphorism: "When you enter the monastery, you leave your body at the gate." That is a complete denial of your humanity. You can't do that; you have to integrate it. Liberation or moksha is what Jesus really means by self-denial. It is an aspiration, yes; but it is also existentially true of you. In the Tibetan tradition, getting beyond karma simply means letting go of your attachments. When you let go of your attachments, and the things that are binding you here, the impermanent things—then you are liberated. Then you have moksha, then you are free of samsara.

L.M.: Reincarnation?

143

W.T.: You're free of the wheel of birth and death, when you no longer have any business here. Karmically, there is nothing holding you back, bringing you back here. Then there are no attachments. Now the problem with this country, this culture.

L.M.: American, Western culture.

W.T.: It is not supportive of spiritual life at this point. And it is radically attached to the impermanent.

L.M.: Society worships the impermanent.

W.T.: You can say it is karma-intensive. So I think that through the sannyasic path, one can achieve liberation. That is what Christ means. The parallel to moksha in Christianity is to lose yourself—that is also the *fanic* consciousness.

L.M.: Of the Sufi, which is the mystical aspect of Islam.

W.T.: Yes, the Sufi annihilation of the self.

L.M.: In order to be really complete and fully conscious?

W.T.: Yes, which means you are removing the obstacles to union with God.

L.M.: We already are that. Although unbeknownst to our conscious selves, because we're unconscious.

W.T.: That's a good point. There is nothing to achieve. It's already achieved. All we have to do is to realize it.

L.M.: So we should not take spirituality or meditation as a kind of achievement test. The Christian sannyasi therefore does have a real understanding of key Hindu concepts such as karma and reincarnation, which are often misunderstood. Isn't reincarnation in the theological sense a lot like the Catholic teaching on purgatory?

W.T.: Yes, reincarnation and purgatory are doing the same work of further education, and refinement, and transformation of the individual. They are leading us to that point where we have the generosity to let go of ourselves. If we die in a state of attachment to these things that are impermanent, then we are not ready for God. In order to have perfect love we must be infinitely, totally free. If we have these attachments, we're not free. We have a divided heart. We are not able to say yes to God at that point. We have to let go of everything else. It can't be done violently. Though some of the saints have done that.

L.M.: Francis tortured Brother Ass, his body.

W.T.: It has to be a gradual transformation for most of us. Still there are these radical moments in our spiritual geography, these monuments of transformation. Saint Francis throwing himself upon the snow, naked—his embrace of the leper and kissing him on the lips. That is a moment of transformation.

L.M.: Has there been such a moment in your life?

W.T.: I've often wondered if I had any compassion; not recently, but in the past. I wondered if I was really capable of compassion and love. I wasn't sure if I was really deluding myself.

L.M.: You were meditating, you were living the sannyasic life. Were you feeling a sense of hollowness?

W.T.: I wouldn't say hollowness. I wasn't really sure of whether I was a loving person, a compassionate person. But I have found that whenever I was confronted with vulnerability in another, my reaching out to them began to show me that I was. I remember seeing once at a lake, a child throw a stone at these two swans, and hit one of them. He didn't kill the swan, but it was injured. And I saw the tremendous distress of its mate.

L.M.: The swan's mate.

W.T.: I felt this incredible sorrow for that being and wanting to lessen its pain and suffering. This happens to me frequently. And I've reached a point

145

where compassion, and the capacity for love and friendship is present—which I have to attribute to God. But I also have a very profound need for solitude, and to maintain my balance. Only if I can be alone with God, then I can really be present to others.

L.M.: Today no one can, or perhaps should be, a cloistered meditator. Whether you are a Christian, Hindu, or Buddhist, you also need to integrate action and contemplation.

W.T. Right.

L.M.: We need to work for justice and a new world. A sannyasi is not indifferent to the world's pain.

W.T.: Not a true one.

L.M.: Or to the anxiety possible in contemporary society.

W.T.: A true sannyasi is a person for others. They have a responsibility to respect the needs of others. For a sannyasi, it is usually spiritual needs, such as giving guidance; hearing another person's story; teaching prayer and meditation; and providing insights into the relationship with the divine—and how to integrate one's life.

L.M.: Brother Wayne, if someone asked you: How I should I meditate? What would you advise them?

W.T.: I would teach them the basic, universal principles of meditation: bodily posture, breath control, and how to quiet the mind through breathing. Perhaps give them a sacred word, or mantra, if they want one. I would also take a more integral, holistic approach to prayer—one must bring the body into it. Walking is a part of my spiritual practice.

L.M.: Walking meditation—very slow walking, as in Buddhist practice—or just walking?

W.T.: I have this practice of what I call a contemplative walk. If you've ever read Thoreau's essay on walking, I recommend it. Walking is very important to me and I do it every day. It's wonderful, it's a contemplative form of prayer for me. A rigorous walk engages your body.

L.M.: And your heart.

W.T.: Your heart—and your mind—and your imagination.

L.M.: Do you feel the love that nature has for us as you walk?

W.T.: Yes, I do, and the integration with nature. I feel nature responding. I have a whole slew of plants in my apartment hermitage in Chicago; they are really a community. One has to be very sensitive and open to understand that level of life. I had this little European cedar which I was very attached to; I had it for a bit more than a year—and then it died. I think one of the reasons it died was because I was going away a lot for weeks at a time. I had been taking good care of it, it was doing great, and all of a sudden, boom.

L.M.: You have envisioned, proposed a universal sannyasic order. What is happening to make your vision a reality?

W.T.: I don't consider myself a founder of the order, but there are a number of Christian sannyasis now in America. Bede and I had talked a number of times about forming an order. He went back and forth with the idea, because the conservative Hindu establishment in India is very much against Christians taking sannyasa. Bede had second thoughts about even calling this sannyasa. But sannyasa is beyond religion. And though much of it may have grown up under the Hindu umbrella, sannyasa transcends Hinduism; it belongs to the collective experience of humanity.

L.M.: Do some of the Hindus also say that sannyasa transcends religion? It's not just Christians who say that.

W.T.: The Hindus have been saying this for thousands of years—that sannyasa is beyond formal religion, because it is focused on the Absolute—which cannot be contained by anyone. So I am encouraging this American group of Christian sannyasis.

L.M.: How many are they?

W.T.: There are five or six at present.

L.M.: Men and women, both?

W.T.: Men and women; there are two Carmelite sannyasi priests in Arizona who have been living the life for over twenty-five years. They're following the teachings of Abishiktananda.

My thought has evolved a lot about sannyasa. I see sannyasa as a meeting place for the religions—a place of dialogue and encounter—and of transformation and spiritual friendships. All religions have the mystical dimension. Spirituality is the real religion of humanity, and the spiritual quest is the focus of the sannyasic calling. Sannyasa can also become a democratizing movement within the church—and within all the religions. So we are talking about a universal order that can bring the religions together.

L.M.: So by democratizing, do you mean de-hierarchizing; and getting beyond the top-down pyramid mode in the Catholic Church?

W.T.: We do have this top-down pyramid mode. But here's the thing about sannyasa. One can become a sannyasi, whether one is a Benedictine or Trappist monk, a priest, or nun, or a lay person. You can be a student, married, single, or whatever.

L.M.: Married sannyasis too?

W.T.: Married people can evolve in their marriage, as they do in India. In its universal form sannyasa is open to anyone who is ready for it.

L.M.: That's great. So you don't have to leave your wife or husband to do this.

W.T.: No, you don't.

L.M.: Your relationship is able to evolve.

W.T.: Your relationship is going to evolve. Love has to become more inclusive; and the problem is that people cling to an exclusive love and call that commitment. They don't realize that love is a school to prepare them to become more inclusive in their love.

L.M.: Making it more universal.

W.T.: Jesus has said: of what value is it that you love only those who love you, and who you are attracted to?

L.M.: That's relatively easy to do, isn't it?

W.T.: Sannyasa can become a way, one way for them to increase their awareness of the divine; and to seek it—to evolve their capacity for love and compassion.

L.M.: Does that mean a couple would gradually let go of their need for sexual expression?

W.T.: Well, it depends. I think they might.

L.M.: Is it an individual matter, and is there to be respect and consideration for the particular couple?

W.T.: It is an individual thing. Certainly sexuality is going to become less and less important. They may choose to express themselves sexually at certain times; but they won't feel the need to do so all the time. They will have such a deep love that it is almost besides the point.

L.M.: Sexual love is not eradicated—it is redirected.

W.T.: No, no, it is not an eradication, it is not a suppression, it is not a denial of it. It is an evolution of it.

L.M.: That is unlike the negative attitudes abut sex some of us grew up with in the church.

W.T.: You leave your body at the gate.

L.M.: Regarding the Shantivanam community in India where Bede lived until his death seven years ago, and where you have spent a good deal of time: How is it contributing to this new sense of community and church?

W.T.: It's a very welcoming environment for people, even though it needs to be more inclusive. It is a part of the Camaldolese Benedictines. They are great people; but it is a very exclusive order.

L.M.: Aren't all the orders exclusive?

W.T.: All the orders are into excluding people—except those that they find acceptable to their charism and their way of life. Although they need to do that to a certain extent to survive, I think they are in sense betraying the gospel. The gospel is about inclusion, not exclusion. This is a lesson that the church has got to learn. Christ was inclusive; he was not exclusive. Still, there is a more inclusive quality at Shantivanam that is open to men and women, Catholics and non-Catholics, Buddhists, atheists.

L.M.: Is there a lay oblate order of Shantivanam?

W.T.: They have lots and lots of oblates. People can come there for long periods and pursue the contemplative experience within the community. It is a light for the world. Though Bede is not physically there with his *darshan*, his presence.

L.M.: Since he died in 1993, it must be harder for the community. It is for any community when the teacher or guru dies.

W.T.: But Shantivanam will continue to have a role.

L.M.: What about loneliness in this battle of the inner life? It is not limited to a sannyasi, or to the spiritual path, though our sensitivity and awareness are heightened by meditation. It's not something to reject. We need to understand it. But it is there.

W.T.: There are moments of it—particularly earlier in my life—and not so long ago. But a year and a half ago I moved into this hermitage, my apartment in Chicago. I was concerned about how I would do being alone, living alone. But I have loved it because it has given me the solitude I need at this point in my life. It is the grace of God that my contemplation, my inner life, is so profound. I feel that support of the divine love pouring into me all the time, and in so many ways—directly, and through other people.

L.M.: Your ongoing friendship with His Holiness the Dalai Lama has come into many of our recent conversations. The disciple Ananda once asked a question of the Buddha to the effect: Is friendship half of the spiritual life? The Buddha replied, "Nay, Ananda, it is the whole of the spiritual life."

W.T.: My experience with His Holiness is again the mystery of the divine workings in our lives. I was in India, and was at a very low point several years ago. I was getting ready to leave India, I'd been there six months.

L.M.: At Shantivanam?

W.T.: Yes, at Shantivanam; I was at this low point while in Benares—Varnarsi—and I bumped into some Tibetan monks who were studying there at the university. They invited me to tea; and one of them kept saying to me: Brother Wayne, you really must go to see His Holiness the Dalai Lama. I had not personally met him, though I had seen him years before in New York. I thought to myself: no, I don't feel that this is the right moment. And then I left India, I didn't go to Dharamsala. When I got to London, Isabel Glover, who is a Sanskrit scholar, said to me: Wayne, you must go and see the Dalai Lama. I was beginning to think it was a conspiracy. She said: he's in England right now. I called and one of the Dalai Lama's representatives there told me they were going to have this intermonastic Buddhist-Christian dialogue at Cardinal Hume's residence. And why don't you come?

So I came, and they put me right at the table—a few feet away from His Holiness. There were about twenty-five or thirty of us. And instantly, there was this connection between the two of us. He communicated to me on a nonverbal level—it was a clear message. He conveyed to me that in our meeting—and through us—Christ and Buddha are meeting. That is what he very clearly communicated to me.

L.M.: But nonverbally?

W.T.: Nonverbally, and very clearly. Now every time we are in each other's presence, we are aware of what each is thinking and feeling. There is just this total acceptance, and this incredible depth of love and affection, and of joy and humor between us. So that friendship is very, very deep; and we are collaborating together in the spirit. It is building the foundation for the next millennium and beyond. It's way beyond us as individuals, do you know what I mean?

L.M.: You have proposed a hunger strike to support Tibet?

W.T.: Well, the hunger strike is aimed really at the Vatican—and its policy of silence on Tibet. Though I realize that the Vatican has legitimate interests in China.

L.M.: The Chinese occupation and genocide in Tibet has been going on there for almost fifty years.

W.T.: Right, for almost fifty years. I think that the gospel and its call to justice has a higher priority—in the mind of the Christ and the spirit, the Trinity—than in the church's interests in China. The church has got to be willing to stick its neck out for justice. This is what is lacking, this is what Christ demands. The silence of the Vatican is therefore intrinsically immoral, because it is a denial of the truth of the gospel. We may have to try something dramatic; we may have to put our lives on the line for the Vatican to wake up from its slumber.

L.M.: So a hunger strike, fasting, is the wake up call?

W.T.: Fasting, a fast.

L.M.: Would that be a large outpouring of people from around the world?

W.T.: Well, I hope so.

L.M.: Interreligious?

W.T.: I don't think it should be focused on one person—it has to be a movement.

L.M.: It's not just your fast.

W.T.: No, no, it should be a group of people. And it should continue until Tibet is free.

L.M.: You're saying that if the church were to speak out now to embrace the cause of the Tibetans—and of the seriously damaged Buddhist culture in Tibet, it would make a difference. Though it still exists; it hangs on in Tibet. Then as a result, Beijing would have to be more forthcoming—if they saw that sign of strength and conviction on Tibet from Christians in the West.

W.T.: I have absolutely no doubt about that. If the Christians in the West—if the Pope would begin to speak out strongly, consistently, and persistently—it would advance support for Tibetans around the world. And a coalition, a nonviolent coalition, would form. China would be confronted with the entire world arrayed against it. Eventually, out of practical necessity they would have to begin to negotiate with the Tibetans. I think that autonomy for that tradition—the culture—would be sufficient.

L.M.: We're talking about the whole of the real, historical Tibet, not just the Tibetan Autonomous Republic, which is much smaller.

W.T.: And let China have control over external affairs and the military.

L.M.: Tibet's people and culture have never sought that in any case.

W.T.: No, it doesn't need it. His Holiness' relation with other governments would have to be controlled by the Tibetans. That whole equation would work for the Chinese; they wouldn't have that drag on them. The Tibet issue is not going to go away. And if the Pope would have a little courage, then everything would come together for the Catholic Church. Its standing in the world would greatly increase. People would look to it more.

L.M.: You make the point in your poem. How did you put it, about our frail Pope?

W.T.: Yes, I said that "Our frail Pope seems to have forgotten the courage of Jesus and Gandhiji." A little courage on his part would spark a transformation of the consciousness of the planet.

L.M.: John Paul II has shown enormous courage with the Solidarity movement in Poland—and the church's role in the end of Communism in central Europe.

W.T.: He played a major role in its unraveling. The thing is, they have to see—and what they don't yet understand—is that Tibet is a test. It is a test which God is giving us. I don't speak metaphorically here: Tibet is a test—conceived by God—for the sake of the whole world. By showing up for the challenge of Tibet, we humans will expand our capacities, our consciousness. If we flunk this test, we may not be worthy to continue as a species.

L.M.: We flunked it with Hitler, as you say.

W.T.: Yes, we flunked it with Hitler. We cannot afford to flunk it this time. We must use any means we can that are moral, nonviolent. And it may take some time to get this off the ground.

L.M.: Would the Dalai Lama support the fast if we had say seventy percent?

W.T.: A seventy percent chance of success, yes. The ultimate success will be the change of the Vatican policy—and for the Vatican to emerge—the Pope to emerge—as a leader in this moral struggle. It would succeed; the Chinese will back down. They may conceive it cynically: that we'll give the Tibetans what they want for a while, but we'll still hold onto Tibet.

L.M.: It will then just be a show.

W.T.: But eventually, the Chinese will themselves be transformed in the process.

L.M.: So, Washington and American business interests don't have to fear the loss of trade with China. Clearly, a moral dimension is required, even though the world of trade and business doesn't go away.

W.T.: But as long as the business community and government ignore the moral issues involved—which are more pressing than the financial benefits—there is blood on that money. And there are karmic consequences to that.

L.M.: How did the call to sannyasa happen to you? How did you hear it, experience it?

W.T.: Well, the call: since I was five years old, there was my wanting to be a priest. No one told me to be that.

L.M.: You were growing up Catholic in Connecticut?

W.T.: Yes, I saw the spiritual journey through my limited knowledge—and that was the priesthood. I always wanted to be a priest. But really, it was my nature as a contemplative—an awakening of the mystic in me—which is in everyone. Everyone is a mystic—whether we accept that or not. It is up to us to accept our vocation as a human being: to be a mystic. It came very early to me, and by the time I was a teenager, it became clearer and clearer. I realized as a teenager that I was a monk, that I was called to that. And later, sannyasa opened up for me.

L.M.: You were a Benedictine for a while.

W.T.: Yes, I was a scholastic at Saint Anselm; and then later, I was at Christ in the Desert monastery in New Mexico. I also went through the Trinitarian novitiate.

L.M.: Those are largely traditional monastic options in the Catholic Church.

W.T.: And then the whole thing of sannyasa opened up for me in my relationship with Bede. Eventually, I did make that commitment. Now if others approach me, I'm very open to initiating others into sannyasa.

L.M.: Is there a formal initiation?

W.T.: Well yes, there is—it's very ancient—I went through a formal initiation.

L.M.: Did you and Bede reorganize that?

W.T.: No, no, no. It was Bede and Abishiktananda who did. It is the ancient sannyasa initiation which is thousands of years old. There are Christian elements in it, in some of the readings, which I would use.

L.M.: What do you look for in those who are ready to consider sannyasa initiation?

W.T.: I am very receptive to people who are coming to the point of awareness and can make that commitment. I would have to discern that, but I wouldn't turn anyone away whom I feel that the spirit is calling. I certainly wouldn't give them psychological testing, and make them wait five years. I have been very critical of that in the church. They need to do some screening; but I think that they often screen out the Holy Spirit in the candidates that God sends. That, they don't want. Jesus says simply three words, "Come follow me." Not, come after you take your psychological exam and have your medical check-up; not, after you get three recommendations and a letter from your pastor, and all the canonical documents and transcripts.

L.M.: You do have at the same time this deep, abiding love for the church. Yet the church shouldn't be put ahead of the gospel—the gospel should be leading the church.

W.T.: Yes, that's the thing. I love the church very dearly. But I am aware that the church needs reform, constantly. The culture of the Catholic Church is very Eurocentric, and is very tied to the Roman Empire. A lot of that culture is not the gospel; a lot of things in that tradition are not good simply because they are traditional.

L.M.: Can you think of one?

W.T.: Yes, the attitude toward women needs to be reexamined, because a lot of that developed through a patriarchal culture. In a very real sense, the first priest was a woman. It was Mary, the mother of God. What does a priest do but make Christ present sacramentally?

L.M.: And Mary did.

W.T.: She made him present through her body. So all that has to be looked at. The church has got to discover within, open up to, and make available to everyone the mystical dimension, the contemplative dimension—which is the human vocation.

L.M.: The sannyasic dimension.

W.T.: The sannyasic dimension. Everybody's got it, everybody's got it. The monk, the mystic, the sannyasi is part of everybody. Everybody is that—that is what we are. And to make that available, and to stress love more, that inclusive love of the gospel. Not simply to function on the level of moral rules, of canon law, and so forth. We need good order in the church. But before that, we need love.

L.M.: I love what you say, that everybody's got it. Everybody's got to get it.

W.T.: Everybody's got to get it, exactly; including, especially, the leaders of the church. Father Bede told me a story about how some contemplative gave a retreat to the Pope and some cardinals at Lent. And he was amazed at their lack of capacity for contemplation. They were always coming and asking for a book to read. So if these are the leaders of the Catholic Church, what's going to happen to the flock? We desperately need an encyclical on prayer, on contemplative life.

L.M.: As a Christian sannyasi, you read, meditate on that book every day, don't you? This book of the self, you're looking at the imprint of God upon us.

W.T.: Right, yes, exactly. The book of nature, the book of creation.

VIPASSANA/THERAVADA BUDDHISM WITH BHANTE GUNARATANA

L.M.: I thought we would start with a question on inner and outer peace. From your perspective, what is Vipassana meditation? And how does this meditation practice help bring about peace in our lives?

B.G.: Vipassana practice is a very involved and deep way of training our mind to reach the very bottom of our mind and our problems. Through vipassana we penetrate all superficiality, and get into the bottom of reality, or truth, that we all experience. We want to remove all the layers of distortion and confusion from our mind to reach reality. Vipassana practice is the method; and its sole purpose is to cleanse the mind of all psychic irritants. We remove the layers of psychic irritants that have accumulated from time immemorial. Inner peace can be achieved only by removing these psychic irritants, because all our chaos, all our problems, all our difficulties—and all kinds of pain, psychological pain, and so forth—stem from our mind.

The Buddha said that he has seen people living in heaven—human beings living there. He said that when they hear, smell, touch, taste, or think of something—then they experience joy, happiness. And they appreciate that. They don't think of those things with any preconceived notions. They just experience them exactly as they are without any biases. In that moment, that individual is in heavenly bliss. On the other hand, somebody can live in hell. That is when someone experiences—or through sight, hearing, listening, tasting, touching, or thinking—they develop a negative attitude such as jealousy, or anger, or confusion. So then, that individual at that moment experiences a very unpleasant experience.

It all comes from the mental attitude, or state of mind. That mental state or attitude is built into that individual's system due to various limitations—one's own limitations as well as those of society, education, and so forth. When we practice mindfulness, then we recognize this. We recognize what is meditation, and what is not meditation. Then we don't nourish the root of unwashed and unwholesome thoughts and experiences. Rather, we deliberately nourish the root of wholesome ones. That is why the Buddha said: there are things we should not develop in our mind; we should not cultivate them. And the things we should cultivate, it is by meditation that we cultivate them. We also learn through mindfulness or vipassana practice that sometimes we are not prepared. And so we perpetuate unwholesomeness, unwholesome things within ourselves.

Buddha taught that all mental states exist for any person at any given moment. But only if the person pays attention to them. If one does not pay attention to certain mental states, then for that instant, at that moment, they do not exist for that individual. We just want to see things exactly as they are. Seeing them exactly as they are is a wholesome way of seeing. That is how we learn to develop inner peace.

Once we have developed peace within ourselves, naturally we will be peaceful, and we will create a peaceful environment. Others will think: Why is this person peaceful, what is his secret? Then, they begin to find out that this person is mindful at all times. A mindful person doesn't say things to hurt others, and doesn't do things to hurt others. He doesn't think unwholesome things in his mind about other people. That person remains peaceful. He learns to practice that golden rule: to love everybody else as himself.

L.M.: Because he is truly finding love in himself?

B.G.: Yes.

L.M.: Before then, he isn't finding it?

B.G.: Before that, if he is loving, he has love only for himself, but it is very superficial. It is not established in wisdom. No one can practice loving-kindness unless the person is wise. One has to be very wise to practice loving-kindness, or *metta*. Because it is the wise person who can understand, and have sympathy for his own suffering—and the suffering of others. He realizes the importance of the practice of loving-kindness. Other people who are not that wise may not cultivate loving-kindness.

Wisdom is not something that we learn from books or education. We may have all kinds of higher knowledge. Sometimes a person can even become like an encyclopedia. He can present facts at his finger tips at any given moment. But when it comes to wisdom, or loving-kindness, he may be very poor. In spite of his knowledge, he has not cultivated the wisdom to see the suffering of all living beings.

Once you understand the suffering of all living beings, then you understand reality. If I do something to hurt myself, I feel pain. And if someone else does something to hurt me, I also feel pain. So everybody is like that—is like myself. Therefore it is foolish for me to hurt someone. We see the depth of pain and suffering through vipassana meditation.

Then one learns to live peacefully, and to create a peaceful environment around him. People will also emulate him. When one is a very peaceful person, then he is very friendly with others. He is full of love, compassion, and understanding. The person will appreciate the ups and downs and the weaknesses of others. Also, due to his wholesome state of being, that person will enjoy good health—good physical health, as well as psychological health.

L.M.: It comes from within oneself rather than from outside.

B.G.: You know we always say that we cannot give others what we don't have, whether it is material or spiritual. Sometimes you may borrow material things. For example, we borrow money from a bank to help somebody, and later we pay it back. But you cannot do that with spiritual things. You have to cultivate them within yourself. Then let that mindfulness emanate from your body. This is what the Buddha called the *Dhammakaya Vipassana*, which is seeing the *dhamma*, or the teaching from within. You can also see from the other person's attitude, and the way they treat other people. This all comes from the practice of vipassana meditation.

L.M.: Vipassana meditation practice is a gradual, gentle approach, in contrast to a certain Zen approach to meditation, or a yogic concentration that requires you to shut out everything. That isn't what really happens in vipassana meditation.

B.G.: No, vipassana is concentration. Without concentration you cannot see things exactly as they are. When you're trying to practice vipassana, you reach a state where hindrances of the mind are suppressed. At that point where your hindrances are suppressed, you gradually gain concentration. One of the factors—one of the mental hindrances—is restlessness and worry. When you remove restlessness and worry, then you gain happiness. Happiness is a precursor to concentration. When you are happy, you gain concentration. But happiness is not excitement.

L.M.: It is not an emotion.

B.G.: No, it's not emotional. It makes you very calm, serene, quiet, composed, and content. That leads to concentration, and that state can arise from the practice of vipassana meditation. So we don't play down concentration, if it is right concentration. Sometimes mindfulness meditation teachers de-emphasize concentration. Instead, we do de-emphasize wrong concentration. Wrong concentration is a kind of concentration where you become attached to it. When you do that wrong kind of concentration, you and the object of concentration become one—and you get stuck there. But when you have right concentration, you would use that right concentration without being attached to it. When you are attached to something, actually you won't get right concentration at all. You have got to be detached, and see exactly what there is. That is the kind of concentration we work for. When you focus that kind of concentration on everything, then you are actually using it as an instrument—as an agent to look into reality in your mind and body.

L.M.: Is that true of the experiences we have during the day, in daily life?

B.G.: Exactly.

L.M.: It is not simply limited to the sitting period, the period of sitting meditation.

B.G.: When you gain deep concentration, you have the peace of that concentration. Sometimes it is for a moment. Momentary concentration is the presence of that deep concentration; in that deep concentration, you can see moments.

L.M.: You see moment to moment?

B.G.: Moment to moment; and then, that moment to moment concentration flows without interruption. And that uninterrupted concentration from moment to moment becomes possible because you have already gained deep concentration.

L.M.: It seems clear that one needs a good or right teacher to learn properly the practice of vipassana meditation. After all, if one wants to learn the guitar, most of us would want a good teacher to learn it. How can we, in our blindness and ignorance, find a good teacher of the Buddha's way, the dhamma? Also, many times a cult of personality gets formed around a teacher, and we are led to think: Well, the teacher is doing it all for me, I don't have to meditate very much.

B.G.: You pose two questions. One is: How does one find a good teacher? The second one is: Is it all right just to blindly trust the teacher? Now let me start with the first question. A right teacher is one who speaks softly, gently, and kindly. He does not try to show his ego. He is very simple and humble. He is the one who tries to understand the student's state of mind. He doesn't get upset when the student asks him a question. He himself is a meditator. And he has a good knowledge of the theory as well as the practice. When you see all of these qualities in one person, you know that he is a good teacher. But you cannot see all of them in one person just in one short association.

L.M.: Or meeting. It takes time?

B.G.: It takes time. At first, you hear about the reputation of the teacher. Sometimes too the teacher is very popular. Then you go to see that teacher, and associate with that teacher for some time. Don't get involved right away. And then, listen to what the teacher says. And using your eyes, watch the teacher's behavior. Then after a while, you realize that you should listen to the teacher's explanation of the teachings. When you listen, you memorize; when you memorize, you begin to assimilate the meaning of what you have memorized. And you can decide whether what you have heard makes sense or not. If it is just superficial, superstitious talk, then you know that is not what you want.

So when you examine—and you see the meaning—then you put it into practice for yourself. When you begin to put those teachings into practice, you begin to see the teacher's sense or meaning. Then you can say that this teacher is a right teacher from your own experience. That is the way to find a good teacher. This is a long process; it is not very easy. Some teachers are wonderful speakers. But when they go back to their houses, there is a discrepancy between their private and public behavior; between what one says, and what one does. That is why sometimes one has to associate with the teacher for some time.

And then, the second question is: Suppose you have found such a good teacher. But you don't do anything, any practice on your part. You think he is wonderful. You just have faith in him; you wash his clothes and make his bed.

L.M.: That's all outward service.

B.G.: And then, because of his grace—that is not going to work. That may help to some extent to win the heart of the teacher, and to learn more of the dhamma. But then, you need to put it into practice. When you put it into practice, then you may get what the teacher has. It is very much like learning any subject—learning to swim, learning to cook, or learning to make a chair. There is a saying that, if an unwise person associates with a wise person all of his life and never learns, he is like a spoon that never tastes soup. You can use the spoon until it wears out. But the spoon never tastes soup. On the other hand, if a wise person associates with a good teacher even for a short period, that person learns to put it into practice, and tastes the dhamma, just like a tongue tastes soup. As soon as you put soup onto your tongue, you can taste it. So that quickly a wise person learns the dhamma by associating with a wise teacher.

L.M.: By putting in their effort, their work, their practice.

B.G.: Exactly, by tasting. We don't believe in just having trust in a teacher; though trust is important too.

L.M.: On a more personal basis, who have been the teachers that have most influenced you in your long years as a monk? You became a monk at the age of twelve, I believe.

B.G.: Yes, at twelve, in Sri Lanka. I had many teachers in monasteries, monks's schools, colleges, and training schools. In all of these places, I met many, many teachers. Very few of them were wonderful.

L.M.: Is there any one teacher who stood out?

B.G.: One teacher, I did not stay with him very long, just two or three years. But the association with him was wonderful. At the time, I was twenty-three or twenty-four.

L.M.: Are there any special or outstanding moments you can recall in your life as a Buddhist monk? For instance, your work with the harijans, or untouchables, in India.

B.G.: Actually, it is all my work with people. Not only with untouchables, but it is with other people—refugees, and people with family problems too. All of this is rewarding for me, because you can see the truth of suffering in all situations. People who are destitute have one kind of suffering or deprivation. And with rich people, I can see their suffering, I can recognize their state of mind. Sometimes, it is working with young people who have a very difficult time dealing with their own life.

L.M.: Where were those refugees you mentioned, in Sri Lanka?

B.G.: No, here in America, in Florida; they were Vietnamese. I was in charge of ten thousand refugees.

L.M.: Was that after the fall of Saigon?

B.G.: Yes, in 1975, I was there with them from May to August.

L.M.: Were you working with a group of monks?

B.G.: With lay people, Buddhists.

L.M.: Do you still hear from some of those refugees?

B.G.: Yes, some of them, occasionally. Of course all of them are totally different now.

L.M.: They're back on their feet again. Another personal question: Bhante Gunaratana, did you always want to become a monk?

B.G.: Yes, I always wanted to be a monk. I always wanted to be a teacher. When I was eight or nine years old, my brother taught me the English alphabet. So one day I was practicing it, and some of my aunts and relatives asked me: What are you doing? I said my brother has taught me some English. Nobody spoke any English. And I told them: I will teach the dhamma in English, I will teach in English, somewhere. And they laughed holding their stomachs as they thought: this is a crazy boy. I don't know why I said that. But that is how I have lived my life for the past forty-two years or so.

L.M.: The Bhavana Society meditation center was established here in West Virginia in 1988, and it is a community for monks, nuns, and even some lay people. There are many lay or secular Buddhists here in the West who practice vipassana meditation. And quite a number of people also come here to Bhavana to learn, and some of them are Christians too. How then, does a person living in society practice vipassana meditation? And too, is enlightenment, or nirvana, possible for the lay vipassana meditator?

B.G.: Any lay person in society, while having families, having children, holding jobs, and being fully engaged in social activities, can practice vipassana meditation. Things that they do in life will be made easier by practicing vipassana meditation. Meditation will reduce their tensions, fears, and excitements for the better—in their family relationships, and in their jobs.

Through mindfulness practice, they will see moment to moment what is really happening. That all their life is like a river; it is a continuous flow. Sight, sound, smell, taste, and touch—all are constantly changing. A person can move and can flow along with these changes, instead of resisting them. They can float on, rather than sink in them.

But first, they have to pay attention to their work. People can spend at least a minute of every hour in mindfulness—in order to relieve tension that builds up in that hour. Secondly, they have to be aware of the impermanence of everything. Third, the object is to gain peace, at least temporarily. And fourth, they unite themselves with the practice of mindfulness meditation.

So by the end of the day, a person will have done ten, twelve, or fifteen minutes of meditation. That means that every hour during the day, take one minute to stop everything—literally, stop everything. And close their eyes and focus. People do not have time and feel pressed; people become workaholics who are more and more interested only in their work. This is a self-perpetuating habit, a vicious cycle. It never ends. It ends only when the person has a heart attack or stroke; when something really bad happens to the person.

L.M.: This one-minute meditation is extremely helpful and practical.

B.G.: This kind of meditation doesn't require a particular place to sit. And people can have a clearer comprehension and competence in their work, when they do this type of meditation.

L.M.: Again, for someone living in the world, is it possible for them to reach enlightenment in this very life?

B.G.: Sure, sure, sure; certainly, they can do it. But gradually, not very quickly. Sometimes people say they can attain enlightenment very quickly.

L.M.: We are very impatient.

B.G.: This sudden attainment of enlightenment seems to work as an incentive for some people. But when they get involved, they realize it does not come that easily. It does not come that quickly. Remember that famous Zen story? Zen people have beautiful stories. A professor goes to a Zen teacher to learn Zen. So the Zen teacher asks the professor to tea. He gave him the cup. And the Zen master was pouring, pouring tea into his cup; it built up, but the teacher did not stop. He kept pouring, pouring, and pouring, and it went onto the saucer. He didn't stop. The tea started to go onto the professor's beautiful, neat trousers. And he got really upset, and was shouting at the teacher to stop. Then the teacher asked: Did you learn Zen?

It means that when the mind is full, we have got to empty it. You have got to uncondition the conditions you already have—before you learn something. You've got to empty, or remove, those unwholesome conditions in order to gain enlightenment. You prepare the soil first. It is like the lotus plant that comes out of the mud. At the very first sign of rain that falls on it, the lotus opens. Other plants in the water do not open like that. Only this one does. Why? Because it has grown so far, so slowly—and so very naturally. It comes to the top, and, when the right moment comes, it opens. Similarly, the attainment of enlightenment requires an enormous amount of temporal experience—of training and practice—in order to receive enlightenment. Sudden attainment may definitely appear to be sudden; as when you see fruit dropping from a tree. It appears to us to happen very suddenly. In fact, the fruit has spent a lot of time on the tree preparing itself, growing, maturing, and ripening. And then, when the right moment came, it dropped.

L.M.: That state of being enlightened, is there any way you can describe it?

B.G.: For instance, we can say that it is peaceful. But someone who knows nothing about peace may wonder what it is. It is serene, calm. There is no ripple of any thought in that state. But explaining it is very difficult.

L.M.: What about love? All of the wisdom traditions, be it Jesus' saying that, "the kingdom of God is within you"; or be it the Hindu Upanishads declaring "thou art that"—all of them seem to point to the very important practice of love.

B.G.: Unless you prepare yourself to experience that love, that kingdom, that peace, those are still just words. People must try within themselves to experience that. To experience that, they must follow certain steps, certain methods, and certain systems. If they don't do that, then they are not experiencing it. It will simply be a theory.

L.M.: What if our meditation practice doesn't lead us to a loving attitude and behavior? Even though I am meditating, I'm still short-tempered, I am noticing and often criticizing the faults of others.

B.G.: We always try to encourage people to look within themselves. Rather than, looking outward and trying to find fault in others, and criticizing others. Sometimes, a teacher may need to criticize students in order to show them the path. To say that: this is not right.

L.M.: Concerning interreligious dialogue, one Buddhist nun has said that, for example, Buddhists and Christians will meet at a conference and they will be saying nice things about one another's religious traditions. But they're thinking: my religion is really the best. Still, it's easy to imagine Buddha and Christ meeting together in a genuine spirit of love. Here at Bhavana, you no doubt have Baptists and Methodists as your neighbors. How can we honestly interact?

B.G.: I'll tell you, I was visiting my students in Brazil, and I came to the airport to find my departure gate. There was a young man, I told him my gate, and he took me there. His father came also, and we were talking very nicely. He said he was a Christian missionary. So I told him: that's very good. You come back and convert these people. Ten years later, I will come back and convert them to Buddhism. So we had a good laugh.

We can have a friendly attitude toward each other—and try to see the truth. The truth doesn't belong to any religion. For instance, when I get angry at anything that another person does, my religion doesn't prevent me saying what I want to say. Similarly, with anybody else, whether Christian, Muslim, Hindu, or whatever, it can be exactly the same. We consider that to be wrong behavior. If on the other hand, I am generous, my being generous does not belong to Buddhism or Christianity.

These are what we call common factors: generosity, compassion, and understanding. If we try to develop these things, then we will not be nitpicky about other religions. Recently, the Pope made a certain statement about Buddhism. And there was a sort of upheaval in some Buddhist countries, some protests. I think that's very sad. We don't need to protest. Because if he made a mistake, it is our duty to point it out to the Pope; I think the Pope would have accepted it. Buddha said: If somebody criticizes the dhamma, or criticizes the Buddha's dispensation, don't get upset. If I get angry because you get angry, I play this interdependent role.

This is how sincerely and honestly we have to work with each other's religions. I tell people that when we started our Buddhist *vihara* in Washington, we did not have many Buddhists. Ninety percent of our supporters were American Christians. There was a Christian minister on our board, I think he was a Methodist. And four Franciscan friars came and helped us with installing our shrine room.

In one Sri Lanka village there is a Catholic church; but there is not one single Catholic living there now. So the bishop appointed a man to be caretaker. He doesn't have any money, he is very poor. So the Buddhists in that area, every Christmas they bring a lot of food and gifts and money to this man. Now Buddhists don't celebrate Christmas. But they know that this man is Christian, and that he celebrates Christmas.

L.M.: That leads us back to the very beginning. About meditation: is not love the whole point of our meditation?

B.G.: Yes, the whole point of meditation. Even materially speaking, biologically speaking, we are all one. We are all made of the same material. We differ from one another only through psychological conditioning. Materially, we are all the same. Our differences are conditional differences. In a spiritual sense also, we become one if we remove these conditions. I may be a Buddhist because I love the dhamma. You are a Christian, because you are brought up in a Christian background. We think that all of us have the same spirit—the spirit of love, of understanding, of compassion.

Sometimes we forget our fundamentals. When we say so and so is a fundamentalist, that is very scary to us. But that is not the real meaning of a fundamentalist. Real, fundamental Christianity is: "Love thy neighbor as thyself." If Christians follow that fundamental—that is a fundamental teaching—there is no way they can fight. There is no way that people can be annoyed or upset when somebody says something to them.

In Buddhist traditions there is the same statement: "Hatred will never be appeased by hatred, but only by love alone." If Buddhists are to be fundamentalists, that is what we should cultivate. Fundamentalism has been totally turned upside down. We must do completely, one hundred percent, wholesome actions. We must bring people back to their real, fundamental, and basic core—the teaching of oneness.

Meditation Resource Directory

A unique and important feature of *Wisdom Roads* is the meditation resource directory that is intended to take the reader's engagement with the eight meditation masters in the book to another, more practical level. There is a multitude of opportunities available for exploring meditation study and practice both in the U.S.A. and Canada as well as in Australia, New Zealand, Brazil, and certain countries in Europe.

For the various meditation wisdom traditions found in the book, a substantial and representative selection of names, addresses, telephone/fax numbers, and especially Internet listings where available is provided.

I recommend a quick click of the mouse to get you on-line with some of the centers' often colorful Web sites that are also outstanding sources of information.

Every reader of *Wisdom Roads* is strongly encouraged to learn first-hand about the rich resources for meditation that these meditation centers and monasteries offer. They are eager to share their insights and knowledge with spiritual seekers regardless of religious affiliation. Through the focus on meditation, these centers are helping bridge the legendary and historic divide between East and West, even as they quietly continue to grow and flourish in today's aptly named global village.

I would also note that in addition to the centers listed here, there are many other notable centers, teachers, and courses of meditation available to the discerning individual. This resource directory is a good place to begin.

CONTEMPLATIVE PRAYER

Holy Cross Abbey, Route 2, Box 3870, Berryville VA 22611-9526; Tel: 540 955-1425/ Fax: 540 955-1356; www.holycrossabbeybrryvlle.org

Our Lady of Angels Monastery, 3365 Monastery Drive, Crozet VA 22932-9802; Tel: 804 823-1452/ Fax: 804 823-6379; www.esinet.net/angels.html

Abbey of Gethsemani, 3624 Monks Road, Trappist KY 40051-6152; Tel: 502 549-3117;Fax: 502 549-4124; www.monks.org

St. Joseph's Abbey, Spencer MA 01562-1233; Tel: 508 885-8700/Fax: 508 885-8701; www.spencerabbey.org

Mount St. Mary's Abbey, 300 Arnold St., Wrentham MA 02093; Tel: 508 528-1282; Fax: 508 528-5360; www.msmabbey.org

Genesee Abbey. P.O. Box 900, Piffard NY 14533-0900; Tel: 716 243-0660/Fax: 716 243-4816; http://web.lemoyne.edu/~bucko/genesee.htm

Mepkin Abbey, 1098 Mepkin Abbey Road, Moncks Corner SC 29461-4796; Tel: 803 761-8509/Fax: 803 761-6719; www.mepkinabbey.org

Monastery of the Holy Spirit, 2625 Hwy. 212 SW., Conyers GA 30208-4044; Tel: 770 483-8705/Fax: 770 760-0989 www.trappist.net

New Melleray Abbey, 6500 Melleray Circle, Peousta IA 52068; Tel: 319 588-2319/Fax: 319 588-4117; www.osb.org/osb/cist/melleray/

Our Lady of Mississippi Abbey, 8400 Abbey Hill, Dubuque IA 52003-9501; Tel: 319 582-2595/ Fax: 319 582-5511; www.osb.org/osb/cist/olm

Assumption Abbey, RR5, Box 1056, Ava MO 65608-9142; Tel: 417 683-5110/ Fax: 417 683-5658

St. Benedict's Abbey, 1012 Monastery Road, Snowmass CO 81654-9399; Tel: 970 927-3311; Fax: 970 927-3399; www.snowmass.org

Abbey of the Holy Trinity, 1250 S. 9500 E., Huntsville UT 84317; Tel: 801 745-3784; Fax: 801 745-6430; www.xmission.com/~hta

Santa Rita Abbey. HC1, Box 929, Sonoita AZ 85637-9705; Tel: 520 455-5595/ Fax: 520 455-5770

Our Lady of New Clairvaux Abbey, P.O. Box 80, Vina CA 96092-0080; Tel: 916 839-2161/ Fax: 916 839-2332; www.maxinet.com/trappist

Redwoods Monastery, Whitethorn CA 95589; Tel: 707 986-7419

Guadalupe Abbey, Box 97, Lafayette OR 97127; Tel: 503 852-7174/ Fax: 503 852-7748; www.trappistabbey.org

CANADA

Abbaye Cistercienne La Trappe d'Oka. 1600 Chemin d'Oka, Oka, Quebec JON 1ED Canada; Tel and Fax:450 479-8361

CHRISTIAN SANNYASA/CAMALDOLESE (BEDE GRIFFITHS)

UNITED STATES

Wayne Teasdale, Catholic Theological Union, 5401 S. Cornell Ave., Chicago IL 60615; Tel: 773 288-6714

New Camaldoli Hermitage, 62475 Coast HWY 1, Big Sur CA 93920-9656; Tel: 831 667-2456 or 3241/fax: 831 667-0209; www.contemplation.com; www.bedegriffiths.com

Incarnation Priory, 1369 La Loma Ave., Berkeley CA 94708; Tel: 510 845-0601/Fax: 510 548-6439; www.contemplation.com

Transfiguration Monastery, 701 NY RTE 79, Windsor NY 13865; 607 655-2366

INDIA

Shantivanam Saccidananda Ashram/Ananda Ashram, Tannirpali PO 639107 Kulittala, Tiruchirapalli District, Tamil Nadu, South India; Tel 91 4323 22260

INTEGRAL YOGA

Satchidananda Ashram Yogaville, Buckingham VA 23921; Tel:800 858-9642/ fax:804 969-1303; www.yogaville.org

Integral Yoga Institute, 227 W. 13 St., New York NY 10011; Tel: 212 929-0586/ Fax: 212 675-3674; www.IntegralYogaofNewYork.org

Integral Yoga Institute, 770 Dolores St. (at 21 St.), San Francisco CA 94110; Tel:415 821-1117; users.aol.com/iyisf/iyi.html

Athens Yoga Center, 263 W. Clayton St. Suite 2, Athens GA 30601; tel: 706 546-4200; www.athens.net/~ayc

JAIN MEDITATION

Jain Meditation International Center, P.O. Box 230244 Ansonia, New York NY 10023-0244; Tel and Fax: 212 362-6483; www.jainmeditation.org

KRIYA YOGA/ADVAITA VEDANTA

Divine Life Church of Absolute Oneness, 5928 Falls Road, Baltimore MD 21209; 410 435-6121; www.divinelifechurch.org

LIGMINCHA TIBETAN BON

Ligmincha Institute, P.O. Box 1892, Charlottesville VA 22903; Tel: 804 977-6161/ fax: 804 977-7020; www.ligmincha.org

Ligmincha Texas Institute of Meditative and Healing Arts, 4219 Richmond, Suite 216, P.O. Box 541479, Houston TX 77254-1479; Tel & Fax: 713 621-7430; www.zenteknet.com/sangha

Ligmincha of California, P.O. Box 1308, Topanga CA 90290; Tel: 323 663-3640 or 310 455-3886; www.ligmincha.org

VIPASSANA MEDITATION

UNITED STATES

Bhavana Society Forest Monastery and Retreat Center, Route 1 Box 218-3, High View WV 26808; Tel:304 856-3241/Fax:304 856-2111; www.bhavanasociety.org

Abhayagiri Buddhist Monastery, 16201 Tomki Road, Redwood Valley CA 95470; Tel:707 485-1630/Fax:707 485-7948; www.abhayagiri.org

Metta Forest Monastery, P.O. Box 1409, Valley Center CA 92082; Tel: 619 988-3474 (bet. 5–6 P.M. PST/6–7 P.M. PDT or leave message; www.here-and-now.org/watmetta.html

Cambridge Insight Meditation Center, 331 Broadway, Cambridge MA 02139; Tel: 617 441-9038/Fax: 617 491-5070; http://world.std.com/~cimc/

International Buddhist Center, 2600 Elmont St., Silver Spring MD 20902-2700; Tel: 301 946-9437; http://members.aol.com/uparatana

International Meditation Center, 438 Bankard Road, Westminster MD 21158; Tel: 410 346-7889; http://ourworld.compuserve.com/homepages/IMCUSA

Ocamora Foundation, P.O. Box 43, Ocate NM 87734; 505 666-2389

Southwest Sangha, Black Range Station, 336 Noonday Canyon Road, San Lorenzo NM 88041; Tel: 505 536-9847

Washington Buddhist Vihara, 5017 16 St. N.W., Washington DC; 202 723-0773; http://vihara.org

The Forest Way Insight Meditation Center, P.O. Box 491, Ruckersville VA 22968; Tel: 804 990-9300/Fax: 804 990-9301; www.forestway.org

CANADA

Arrow River Community Center, Box 2, RR7, Site 7, Thunder Bay, Ontario P7C 5V5, Canada; Tel: 807 933-4434; www.baynet.net/~arcc

Birken Forest Monastery, P.O. Box 962, Princeton, British Columbia V0X 1W0 Canada; Tel: 250 295-3263; http://homepage.oanet.com/andyshaw/bfmpage.htm#BirkenForestMonastery

IRELAND

Passaddhi, Marjo Osterhoff, Leitrim Beg, Adrigole, Beara, Co. Cork, Ireland; Tel: 011 353 27 60223/Fax: 353 27 60209; www.midnet.ie/beara/passaddhi.html

ITALY

Monastero Buddhista Santacittarama, Via Delle Prata 22, Lacalita, "Le Brulla" 02030 Frasso Sabino, Brulla, Rieti, Italy; 39 765 872186

UNITED KINGDOM

Amaravati Buddhist Monastery, Great Gaddesden, Hemel Hempstead, Hertfordshire HP1 3BZ England UK; 44 01442 842455/843239/843721;

Aruna Ratanagiri Harnham Buddhist Monastery, Harnham, Belsay, Northumberland NE20 0HF; 44 01661 881612/Fax: 01661 881 019; www.ratanagiri.org.uk

Cittaviveka Chithurst Buddhist Monastery, Chithurst, Petersfield,

Hampshire GU31 5EU; 01730 819986;Fax: 01730 812334
Devon Vihara Hartridge Buddhist Monastery, Upottery, Honiton, Devon
EX14 9QE; tel: 01404 89 1251/Fax: 01404 89 0203

Santidhamma Forest Hermitage, Lower Fulbrook near Sherbourne,
Warwickshire CV35 8AS, England; Tel/Fax: 44 01926 624385; www.users.
zetnet.co.uk/phrakhem/

AUSTRALIA

Bodhinyana Monastery, Lot 1, Kingsbury Drive, Serpentine, Western
Australia 6125; Tel: 61 8 4525 2420/Fax: 61 8 9525 3420; www.iinet.net/
au/~ansonb/bswa

Dhammasara Nuns Monastery, Lot 233, Reen Road, Gidgegannup, Western
Australia 6083; (no phone)

NEW ZEALAND

Bodhinyanarama Forest Monastery, 17 Rakau Grove, Stokes Valley,
Wellington, New Zealand; Tel: (04) 563-1793/Fax: (04) 563-5125; http://
yourname.co.nz/wwebz/bodhinet.htm

WORLD COMMUNITY OF CHRISTIAN MEDITATION

UNITED KINGDOM

WCCM International Centre, 23 Kensington Square, London W85HN,
England UK; Tel: 44 171 937-4679/Fax: 44 171 937-6790; www.wccm.org

Christian Meditation Centre, The Hermitage, Monastery of Christ the King,
29 Bramley Road, Cockfosters, London N144HE England UK

UNITED STATES

Christian Meditation Center, 193 Wilton Road West, Ridgefield CT 06877 Tel: 203 438-2440

Christian Meditation Center, 1619 Wight St., Wall NJ 07719; Tel: 732 682-6238/Fax: 732 280-5999

Christian Meditation Center, 1080 W. Irving Park Road, Roselle IL 60172; Tel and Fax: 630 351-2613

The Cornerstone Center, 1215 E. Missouri Ave., Suite A100, Phoenix AZ 85014-2914; Tel: 602 279-3454/ Fax: 602 957-3467

John Main Institute, 3727 Abbeywood, Pearland TX 77584

IRELAND

Christian Meditation Centre, 4 Eblana Ave., Dun Laoghaire, County Dublin, Ireland; Tel: 353 1 280-1505; fax: 353 1 280-8720

ITALY

Centro di Meditazione Cristiana, Abazzia di San Miniato al Monte, Via Delle Porte Sante 34, 50125 Florence (FI) Italy; Tel and Fax: 39 055 2476302

AUSTRALIA

Christian Meditation Center, P.O. Box 66390, St. Kilda Road Central, Victoria 3004 NSW, Australia; Tel and Fax: 61 7 3300-3873

CANADA

Christian Meditation Community, P.O. Box 552, Station NDG, Montreal,

Quebec H4A3P9, Canada; Tel: 514 766-0475/Fax: 514 937-8178
BRAZIL

Comunidade Mundial para Meditação Crista, Rua Joao Porto 283-Centro, Jacarei SP Brasil Cep 12300-000; Tel/Fax: 012 352-8812; http://sites.uol. com.br/wccm

GERMANY

Zentrum für Christliche Meditation, Postfach 122045, 68071 Mannheim; Tel: 49 171 268-6245 http://home.t-online.de/home/WCCM-D/haupt.htm

THE TEACHERS

Laurence Freeman OSB leads Christian meditation retreats and travels extensively as spiritual director of the World Community of Christian Meditation that was founded by his spiritual mentor, John Main OSB. Father Laurence, a native of Britain, lives at a Benedictine monastery in London. He also teaches regularly at the WCCM center in Florence, Italy.

Swami Satchidananda is an internationally respected teacher, author. and speaker who introduced the Integral Yoga teachings to the West over thirty years ago. He received initiation into Sannyasa by his guru Swami Sivananda in India in 1949. A native of South India, he is the founder and resident spiritual guru of Satchidananda Yogaville Ashram in Buckingham County, Virginia.

Tenzin Wangyal Rinpoche is one of the leading teachers of Bon Dzogchen meditation in the West. He travels extensively to give retreats and workshops on Bon in the U.S., Europe, Asia, and Mexico. He received the doctorate of Geshe degree at the Bonpo Monastic Center in Dolanji HP, India. His teachers in the Bon and Buddhist traditions include Lopon Sange Tenzin, Lopon Tenzin Namdak Rinpoche, and Geshe Yangdrung Namgyal. Tenzin Wangyal, who is of Tibetan heritage, is the founding president and resident Lama of Ligmincha Institute in Charlottesville, Virginia.

Edward McCorkell OCSO, has been teaching contemplative prayer to monks, lay retreatants, and others for many years. He has been very involved in the intermonastic dialogue with Buddhist and Hindu monks and nuns. He has served as abbot of monasteries in Virginia and in Chile. A South African native, Father Edward, who has been a Cistercian monk for over fifty years, lives at Holy Cross Abbey in Virginia.

Swami Shankarananda is a respected teacher and author of books on Kriya Yoga/Advaita Vedanta. He is the founder and spiritual guide of the Divine Life Church of Absolute Oneness in Baltimore. He received initiation into the

Swami Order from his guru, Swami Premananda. He divides his time between Baltimore and the Shenandoah Valley of Virginia.

Shree Chitrabhanu has been the leading exponent of Jain meditation teachings in the West since 1971. He has now founded seventeen Jain temples in North America. He was formerly a Jain monk in India for many years; he also observed a vow of silence for some time. A native of India, Shree Chitrabhanu regularly writes, lectures, and teaches about Jain meditation. He lives with his wife in New York City and in Bombay, India.

Wayne Teasdale, a Connecticut native, is a Christian sannyasi, and he regularly gives retreats and lectures on the contemplative, mystical life. He serves on the board of the Parliament of World Religions and he is the coordinator of the Bede Griffiths International Trust. He received a Ph.D in mystical theology from Fordham University in 1986. His spiritual mentor, Bede Griffiths, initiated him into Christian Sannyasa at Shantivanam ashram in South India in 1989. Brother Wayne lives in Chicago where he is adjunct professor at Catholic Theological Union, DePaul University, and Columbia College.

Bhante Henepola Gunaratana is one of the most internationally respected teachers of Vipassana meditation. He continues to travel the world in his mission to spread the Buddhadhamma. His preceptor was Ven. Kiribatkumbure Sanuttara Mahathera. He worked for the Mahabodhi Society among the "harijans" (the untouchable caste) in India for several years. He has a Ph.D in philosophy from American University where he served as Buddhist chaplain. He is past president of the Washington Buddhist Vihara. Bhante Gunaratana, a native of Sri Lanka, is the founder and resident director of the Bhavana Society Forest Monastery and Retreat Center in West Virginia.

BIBLIOGRAPHY

Laurence Freeman

Common Ground: Letters to a World Community of Meditators. New York: Continuum International, 1999.

Web of Silence. New York: Continuum, 1998.

The Selfless Self. New York: Continuum, 1998.

The Light Within: The Inner Path of Meditation. New York: Continuum, 1998.

John Main

Moment of Christ. New York: Continuum, 1998.

Heart of Creation. New York: Continuum, 1998.

The Cloud of Unknowing and the Book of Privy Counseling (anonymous), tr. by William Johnston. Garden City, NY: Image Books/Doubleday, 1996 (reissue).

The Way of the Pilgrim and the Pilgrim Continues His Way, ed. by R. M. French. San Francisco: HarperCollins, 1991 (reprint).

Swami Satchidananda

To Know Your Self: The Essential Teachings of Swami Satchidananda. Buckingham, VA: Integral Yoga Publications, 1988 (rev).

The Yoga Sutras of Patanjali. Buckingham, VA: Integral Yoga Publications, 1990 (rev).

The Living Gita; The Complete Bhagavad Gita: A Commentary for Modern Readers. Buckingham, VA: Integral Yoga Publications, 1998 (rev).

Tenzin Wangyal Rinpoche

The Tibetan Yogas of Dream and Sleep. Ithaca, NY: Snow Lion Publications, 1998.

Wonders of the Natural Mind: The Essence of Dzogchen in the Native Bon Tradition of Tibet. Barrytown, NY: Station Hill Press, 1993.

Edward McCorkell (Contemplative Prayer)

Thomas Keating, *Open Heart, Open Mind.* New York: Continuum, 1992 (reissue).

Thomas Merton, *New Seeds of Contemplation.* New York: New Directions, 1960.

Thomas Merton, *The Asian Journal.* New York: New Directions, 1969.

Swami Shankarananda (as Peter Achariya)

Mystic Easter. Baltimore: Darshan.

Spiritual Perfection. Baltimore: Darshan, 1984.

Paramahansa Yogananda

Autobiography of a Yoga. Los Angeles: Self-Realization Fellowship, 1946, 1993 (12th Edition).

Swami Premananda

Eight Upanishads. Washington, DC: Mahatma Gandhi Memorial Foundation, 1989.

Shree Chitrabhanu

Ten Days Journey into Self. New York: Jain Publications, 1998 (rev.).

The Miracle is You. New York: Jain Publications, 1996 (rev.).

Realize What You Are: The Dynamics of Jain Meditation. Fremont, CA: Asian Humanities Press, 1995 (rev.).

Psychology of Enlightenment: Meditations on the Seven Energy Centers. Fremont, CA: Asian Humanities Press, 1994 (rev.).

Wayne Teasdale

The Mystic Heart: Discovering a Universal Spirituality in the World's Religions. Novato, CA: New World Library, 1999.

The Community of Religions: Voices and Images of the Parliament of the World's Religions, ed. with George M. Cairns. New York: Continuum, 1996.

Toward a Christian Vedanta: The Encounter of Hinduism and Christianity According to Bede Griffiths. Bangalore, India: Asian Trading Pub., 1987.

Essays in Mysticism: Explorations into Contemplative Experience. Lake Worth, FL, 1985 (rev.).

Bede Griffiths

Universal Wisdom: A Journey Through the Sacred Wisdom of the World. San Francisco: HarperCollins, 1994.

The New Creation in Christ: Meditation and Community. London: Darton Longman Todd, 1992.

The New Vision of Reality: Western Science, Eastern Mysticism, and Christian Faith. London: Springfield, IL: Templegate Publishers, 1989.

Bhante Henepola Gunaratana

Mindfulness in Plain English. Boston: Wisdom Publications, 1993.

The Path of Serenity and Insight: An Explanation of the Buddhist Jhanas. Moltilal Banarsidass Pub., 1992.

THE AUTHOR

Lawrence G. Muller is a writer, journalist, and long-term meditator. He is the recipient of the Being Together Conferences (1991–1999) Award for his contributions to Interreligious Dialogue. He worked as a religion journalist for several years at a daily newspaper in Virginia. He is a lay oblate of New Camaldoli Hermitage in California, and he has visited numerous monasteries and ashrams in North America, Europe, and India. He received his B.A. in English Literature/Humanities from Harpur College, Binghamton University. A New York City native, Lawrence presently resides in the Shenandoah Valley of Virginia.